THE ROYAL EN
HOU

THE QUEEN, 31 JANUARY 1891

SULLIVAN's

IVANHOE

Published in Great Britain by the Sir Arthur Sullivan Society
in September 2007.

Edited for the Sir Arthur Sullivan Society by D.J. Eden.

All pictorial material in this publication has been obtained
from non-copyright sources.

The Sullivan Society extends its thanks to the following for their help in
providing pictorial material and other valuable assistance:

Mr Tim Sturgis, Miss Miranda Seymour,
Mr Julian Seymour, Mrs Anne Porter,
Mr Robin Gordon-Powell, Mr Vincent Daniels,
Mr Melvin Tarran, Mr William Parry, Mr Simon Moss.

Published by the Sir Arthur Sullivan Society
At 55 Radwinter Road, Saffron Walden,
Essex, CB11 3HU.

Martin Yates
Chairman
Ikilty37@aol.com

Paperback ISBN 978-0-9557154-0-2

CONTENTS

HILDA THUDICHUM (REBECCA)

ESTHER PALLISER (ROWENA)

LUCILLE HILL (ROWENA)

BEN DAVIES (IVANHOE)

MARGARET MACINTYRE
(REBECCA)

THE MAKING OF IVANHOE

By David Eden

While he rapidly abandoned any ambitions he may have had in the field of symphony and concerto, Sullivan persisted through a long and arduous course in the matter of opera. The great bulk of his output is operatic or theatrical, and even his choral works are cast in dramatic form. As his disagreements with Gilbert make clear he was dissatisfied with the Savoy formula, constantly seeking to expand into the emotional territory of opera in the ordinary sense. His inability to reach a satisfactory outcome in this respect was responsible for the events leading up to the composition of *Ivanhoe*, just as the fate of *Ivanhoe* itself led to his return to the Savoy.

Sullivan received the first draft of Julian Sturgis' *Ivanhoe* libretto at the end of July 1889, having dined with D'Oyly Carte and Sturgis on 5 June. Composition was begun on 17 May 1890, aided by regular visits from Sturgis: 'worked with him at all sorts of details in the opera,' wrote Sullivan. 'He is quick at seeing my meaning and falls into it with kindly readiness.' (1) The last note was put to the score on 13th December 1890, later than intended, but not unduly so for a work of such length (3 hours). These, at least, are facts. Almost everything else one reads about *Ivanhoe* belongs to the realm of make-believe, as the work is described as a damp squib or a shattering disaster according to the predilections of the writer. Even commentators who were present at the first night and lived through the subsequent events seem to have had little idea of what actually happened to the opera. One persistent myth we may scotch at once: Sullivan did not express his dislike of *Ivanhoe* to Reginald de Koven, or say 'A cobbler should stick to his last.' At least he must have done so from beyond the grave, because the alleged remark would have been made in 1910 – ten years after his death. (2)

The opera house project seems to have originated in the mind of D'Oyly Carte as a way of providing enhanced accommodation for operas by Gilbert and Sullivan, thereby keeping them ahead of the field, as represented by Alfred Cellier's enormously successful *Dorothy* (1886). On 13 February 1888 he, Carte, wrote to Sullivan urging him to secure the co-operation of Gilbert in making a new start:

> If you wish the scheme to go through you will not delay writing to Gilbert at once and putting your views with that decisive clearness which is always at your command. If I do not let the Savoy to a good tenant, or sell it, our scheme cannot I fear go through at all. Gilbert is not fully reconciled to the plan, but he is I think in that frame of mind in which your letter would probably decide him in favour of it . . . (3)

In the mind of Sullivan at least these future operas were to have a more substantial musical content than the Savoy series, even if not wholly sung. Building work had already begun when Gilbert refused to become involved - no doubt the initial discussions with him had resulted in the usual misunderstandings. (4) Instead of abandoning his plans Carte transferred his ambitions to English opera in general, and in due course it became established that Sullivan would write an opera to inaugurate the new house, which was to be run on principles unlike those obtaining at the Savoy.

The Savoy practice was to allow a newly produced work to run more or less as long as it would return a healthy profit, then abandon it with no specific intention of revival. At the new theatre the initial run was meant to pay for production expenses, after which the opera would become part of a repertory to be built up by a succession of new works. Sullivan's views on the matter had already been made clear some years before in an interview with the *Musical World*:

> . . . . But many conditions are required for success in operatic management. I apprehend that a successful opera must be played every night to make money. Life is too hurried now to calculate over one opera on Mondays and Wednesdays, another on Tuesdays and Thursdays, and another on Fridays and Saturdays. People will not, I think, do this; and then, if you run your opera every night, you require a double cast of singers. Good singers will hardly consent to sing through a grand opera every night. Very few have sufficient physical power, and even they would be wise not to exert it. (5)

We are now in a position to understand the proper nature of the 155 performances received by *Ivanhoe* on its first production. This was a run of exactly six months (31st January to 31st July 1891), representing not the absolute limits of the opera's drawing power, but a planned season during which it was to recover expenses. Irving's *Macbeth* production, for which Sullivan had written the music, was still drawing full houses when withdrawn after a season of six months (150 performances) in 1889; (6) Sullivan's ballet *Victoria And Merrie England* similarly ran for six months (155 performances) in 1897. The last night of *Ivanhoe* in July 1891 was also the last night of the Covent Garden season, after which musical London traditionally went on holiday. 'The brilliant campaign at Covent Garden,' said *The Era*, 'has mainly absorbed the public interest in operatic matters, but other events of importance may also be chronicled - the 300th night of *La Cigale* [*Audran*] on Friday, for example; the success attending Sir Arthur Sullivan's *Ivanhoe* . . . (7)

The novelty and ambition of the *Ivanhoe* scheme made it a natural focus of press attention. Events at the opera house were reported regularly, and from these it is possible to build up a detailed picture of the decisions and indecisions by which the final outcome was reached. Carte should not be accused of failing to plan ahead. He commissioned at least three operas from British composers (Cowan, McCunn, and Goring Thomas) besides buying the rights to two continental works - Bemberg's *Elaine*, and Messager's *La Basoche*. In theory these, together with *Ivanhoe*, should have been enough to provide him with a repertory; in practice it was precisely the attempt to establish it in repertory that led to the downfall of *Ivanhoe*. The following narrative has been abstracted from the pages of the *Pall Mall Gazette*, a paper of first-rate editorial quality which took a particular interest in the progress of the opera. As Sullivan had foreseen, *Ivanhoe* was performed by two casts of principals because of the strain imposed on the voices by the constant repetition of demanding music. (8) Besides adding to running expenses these casts were necessarily not of equal merit, resulting in lower attendances on those nights when the second or inferior cast was performing.

After a brilliant opening night (31st January 1891) *Ivanhoe* ran to full houses for several weeks at high ticket prices. The Royal English Opera House, as the new building was known, was the largest theatre in London, holding 2300 people and about £670 when full (the Savoy held 1150 and £350). (9) Responding to much adverse comment on his high prices, including the music hall song reproduced on page 62, Carte lowered them on 25th February from 3/6d to 3/- in the pit. At the same time the first reports began to circulate of an opera by a German composer to be produced as a successor to *Ivanhoe*. On 20th March the German composer was revealed as

Herman Bemberg (actually a Frenchman) and the opera as *Elaine*, based on *The Idylls Of The King*:

> It is now said that Mr Carte will close his Royal English Opera House after the present season. What he will do when he reopens in the autumn is not as yet definitely settled. One of the difficulties in connection with M. Bemberg's opera - which has been described as *Romeo and Juliet* over again - was the selection of artists, and a condition that M. Bemberg should be at liberty to produce his opera at Covent Garden with Jean de Reszke. This latter provision has, we understand, been arranged. Should M. Bemberg's opera not be sufficiently forward, it is expected that Mr Carte will fall back on a new opera which Mr Hamish McCunn has undertaken to furnish, the libretto of which will be by a well known novelist [*Andrew Lang*] and a well known journalist [*Joseph Hatton*] who have previously collaborated. The subject is said to be an essentially modern one. Should the negotiations now pending be successful, Mr Carte may open his season with a 'triple' attraction, *Ivanhoe* being given two nights a week. M. Bemberg's opera on two nights, and Mr Hamish McCunn's opera on the other evenings. (10)

At the beginning of April audiences for *Ivanhoe* had evidently fallen to an extent sufficient to fuel speculation about the opera house's future: 'Mr Carte will have to face the fact that English opera cannot remain his mainstay' (3rd April). By 10th April there was talk of alternating *Ivanhoe* with *The Flying Dutchman*. However the 24th April saw full houses for *Ivanhoe* after the end of Lent; on 28th April *Ivanhoe* was 'flourishing like the green bay tree just now, but in due course we may expect to see it alternated with an English version of the opera above referred to.' The 'opera above referred to' was Messager's *La Basoche*, purchased by Carte in March 1891 after production at the Opéra Comique (Paris) on 30th May 1890. On 2nd May 1891 the pairing of *Ivanhoe* and *La Basoche* was said to be due 'in about a month.' Rehearsals for *La Basoche* began on 5th June, 'but its present run will, however, be of short duration, for current arrangements point to a probable vacation at the opera house from the last week in July until the end of September. During this period the rehearsals of *Elaine* will be pushed on . . . . *Ivanhoe* has been playing to good houses lately, the return of Miss Macintyre (Rebecca) having had a stimulating effect on bookings' (12th June). On 11th July *La Basoche* was still said to be in active rehearsal, and there was now talk of keeping the theatre open during the summer vacation:

> So good have been the takings at the Royal English Opera House during the past few weeks that it is quite possible that the theatre will not close for the contemplated vacation. The reduction of the charge for seats to the ordinary theatre level is largely accountable for this desirable improvement.

Finally, on 25th July:

> Mr D'Oyly Carte has wisely decided to postpone the production of *La Basoche* until the end of September or the first week in October. Meanwhile the English Opera House will close for two months' vacation today week, affording a hard-earned rest to the members of the *Ivanhoe* company. It is possible that *Elaine* will be still further postponed.

In this way the first six months of the production came to an end. The *Pall Mall Gazette* obviously took its information from someone in Carte's office, and the statements about financial matters may be optimistic; nevertheless the opera house had survived as a going concern. The proposed production of alternatives to *Ivanhoe* had not proved necessary, and Carte ended by doing what he had intended all along, namely running *Ivanhoe* for a season before including it in repertory with another work. It seems that Carte had contracted his two *Ivanhoe* casts precisely for the initial six-month period. He now asked them to hold themselves ready for the autumn revival, but in accordance with contemporary practice paid them no retaining fee - an omission whose consequences will become apparent.

The interest of the *Pall Mall Gazette* in affairs at Shaftesbury Avenue did not diminish with the close season. Regular reports continued to appear, including the following on 29th August 1891:

> Mr D'Oyly Carte is expected to return to London at the end of next week, and very little time will be lost before the rehearsals of *La Basoche* are resumed. The production of *Elaine* will then be considered, but whether it will see the light before Christmas will largely depend on the drawing power of the new light opera, combined with *Ivanhoe*, to which, by the bye, Miss Macintyre will not return. (11) In the meantime Mr F.H. Cowen is making satisfactory progress with the opera [*Signa*] which he is writing to a libretto by Mr Gilbert à Beckett, which is based on a dramatic English novel. [*by Ouida*] Mr Cowen's opera is expected to follow *Elaine*, and that being so, the date of Mr Hamish McCunn's *Cleopatra* is very uncertain. When we last heard of Mr McCunn he was waiting for the completion of certain portions of the libretto to enable him to proceed.

On the face of it Carte appears to have had a healthy choice of operas for production. In fact only *La Basoche* among the impressive list was really in existence. Cowen did not complete *Signa* until January 1892, having been commissioned by Carte on 14th May 1890; (12) Bemberg finished *Elaine* in October 1891, but production was hampered by lack of a prima donna; Hamish McCunn never wrote an opera on Cleopatra (unless Jeanie Deans were she). Goring Thomas, whom Carte had commissioned about February 1891, was said on 12th June to have chosen a subject of the time of Louis XIV, 'but is sadly in want of a libretto.' Thomas wished this libretto to be written in French, his preferred language, but in the autumn of 1891 he began to show the symptoms of mental instability that led to his suicide on 20th March 1892. There was no true prospect of a work from him. Stanford, who wrote music in full score before breakfast, would have been a reliable contributor, but was not approached. Edward German offered his services, and was turned down.

With two of his commissioned operas definitely *hors concours*, Carte's room for manoeuvre was less than he might have wished. Nevertheless *La Basoche* was a known quantity, having been successful in Paris. Taken together with the already-proven *Ivanhoe*, there seemed no reason why these works should not keep the theatre open until the next generation of operas was to hand. The rehearsal period seems to have been longer than anticipated, but eventually all was ready for an opening at the beginning of November. *La Basoche* was given on Wednesday 4th November 1891 to ecstatic press reviews and great enthusiasm from a less than full audience - both Carte and Sullivan thought the reopening of the theatre had been insufficiently advertised. In accordance with the next stage of the plan *Ivanhoe* was introduced on Friday 6th, and then played on 7th, 9th, 12th. 13th and 18th November. Ticket prices for *Ivanhoe* in the cheaper parts of the house were 1/ - higher than for *La Basoche* - and the audiences simply did not turn up. (13) For all his forward planning Carte had failed to anticipate what the actual effect of his repertory policy would be. *Ivanhoe* had, for the time being at least, exhausted its market in the six months to July. Now, in November, it was pitted at higher ticket prices against a hugely praised new production, with the only possible outcome - anybody who wanted to go to the Royal English Opera at all went to *La Basoche*, leaving *Ivanhoe* without an audience and Carte without the means to pay his performers. *La Basoche* itself did not take really adequate sums.

Carte's position was now highly embarrassing. Having left his double *Ivanhoe* casts unemployed and unpaid from August to November, he had engaged them for a season, meaning he would have to pay them, even if they sang to an empty auditorium. Sullivan, according to his diary, urged him either to close the opera house or do *The Flying Dutchman* at once. In his autobiography Sir Henry Wood, who was répétiteur at the Royal English Opera, says he actually began to rehearse Eugene Oudin (Sullivan's Templar) for the part of the Dutchman. (14) Carte chose the former course. He declared the season over, and attempted to terminate the contracts of all performers, including those in *La Basoche*. The *Pall Mall Gazette* of 21st November 1891 describes the situation:

> The sudden withdrawal of *Ivanhoe* from the bills of the Royal English Opera has surprised no-one, and it is generally understood that the production of Sir Arthur Sullivan's grand opera has placed Mr D'Oyly Carte on the wrong side of the balance sheet, the total loss being said to have been £25,000. The stoppage has been of serious consequence to many of the artists engaged, who are now under a fortnight's notice to consider themselves out of the Royal English Opera company. At the meeting held last Monday [*16 November*] Mr Carte put the situation before the company and appealed to them to consider the great loss he had sustained by playing the opera. This is very reasonable, but on the other hand the situation of the principal artists is even more unsatisfactory. For three months they have held themselves in readiness to resume their duties at the Opera House, without salary, refusing concert engagements and other work, only to find that after a fortnight's run *Ivanhoe* is no good. Then comes a meeting and a fortnight's notice just at the time of the year when most concert arrangements have been made. It can be well understood that, in acting for the best, Mr Carte has caused a great deal of dissatisfaction.

Here lies the root of all the stories about the disastrous failure of *Ivanhoe*. Carte's precipitate action traumatised his cast, and bewildered the public. Some of the disaffected performers, apparently led by the bass Norman Salmond, were disinclined to go quietly. A legal dispute arose, referred to by Carte in a letter printed in the *Pall Mall Gazette* of Thursday 26th November:

> A paragraph calculated to convey a somewhat erroneous impression appeared in the *Pall Mall Gazette* of Saturday last [*21ˢᵗ November*] giving some account of what took place at a private meeting held on Monday the 16th inst. to which the press were not invited, and at which those present undertook to consider all that passed there as confidential. As, however, such a paragraph has appeared, I must ask you to allow me to say that I made no "appeal" to the artists for any concession to me. I informed them that notwithstanding the great success of the *Basoche* it was impossible at the reduced prices which I had found myself obliged to put up in order to fill the cheaper parts of the house, to continue the enormous expense then going on, and that therefore I had to terminate the season. I also informed them that I might reopen on an entirely different basis and play the *Basoche* for a run. I explained that of course it would be better for those concerned in the piece to continue without a break, and that I was disposed to do so if the artists of the company were agreed that they would not raise any question that their season engagements were continuing if the theatre were kept open without a break; that I should be entirely unable to do so, and could not attempt it if there were to be any disputes on this point; that if the theatre were closed then all artists, those playing in the *Basoche* as well as the others, the orchestra and the army of chorus supers, stage hands and employees would be out of employment, which many, especially the smaller salaried people, could ill afford. I explained that it was a matter of absolute indifference to me except for the throwing out of work of so many people, and that the decision rested with them. Without going further into what took place at the meeting, I may say that the response of the artists was quite satisfactory. Difficulties, however, have since arisen, into the nature of which I need not go publicly. I am sorry that someone has betrayed the confidence which they all voluntarily undertook to respect. I think the matter is hardly one which concerns the public, but the statement having been made, I feel the above explanation is necessary.

This letter is notable for making no direct reference to *Ivanhoe*; but Carte seems to be saying - and seems always to have believed - that his problems arose from low tickets prices not poor attendances. The threat of legal action was not removed, and he terminated his season altogether on Saturday 28th November 1891. The *Pall Mall Gazette* expressed itself satisfied that he had taken the 'only possible' course of action under the circumstances, and he himself wrote a further letter of explanation, published in the *Pall Mall Gazette* on 30th November:

> I shall be obliged if you will allow me to explain that it is in consequence of certain legal disputes that I have found it necessary to terminate the Royal English Opera season, to close the theatre, and stop the "run"; but that should the disputes referred to be adjusted, which I trust may prove to be the case, in a few days I may probably be able to arrange to recommence the performances, of which due notice will be given. May I beg that all those who have written to me on this subject will kindly take this as a reply to their communications, the number of which renders it impracticable to answer them individually.

In addition to those printed by the *Pall Mall Gazette*, letters from Carte appeared in the *Times* on Saturday 28th November, and again, at length, on Thursday 3rd December. The letter of 3rd December does not say much about the dispute which had closed the theatre, but it does provide some useful background information. Cowen's *Signa* is the opera which is 'even now not completed.':

> I trust I shall not be considered as carping at the uniformly friendly and generous notices given by the press to *The Basoche* if I refer to some observations made in certain journals as to my performing an opera by a French composer at the "English" Opera House. Surely there can be no reason why operas by foreign composers played in English should not be given at the English Opera. At the Royal "Italian" Opera many of the works given are by French and German composers. At the Grand National Opera of Paris many operas are given in the language of the country in which they are played. In the repertoire of my late regretted friend Mr Carl Rosa's "English Opera" Company there were and still are *Faust*, *Romeo*, *Carmen*, *Lohengrin*, and a host of operas by foreign composers and authors translated into and played in English. Music speaks a language intelligible to all civilised nations. It is quite true that in my announcement of the opening of my theatre I referred especially to the number of English composers, authors, and singers that there are now, and in this way emphasised the national character the theatre was expected to develop, but I nowhere stated that I should only play works by English composers. I might almost as well have declined to engage American singers; but I could scarcely have formed so good a company as I did without Mr Oudin, Miss Palliser, Mr Bispham, Miss Groebi, Mr Avon Saxon, Miss Henson, and Miss Lucile Hill, all of whom are from the United States. I certainly intended to give the preference to works by English composers and authors; but, if the English composers are not ready - and the first of a series of operas by English composers to be written under contracts with me is even now not completed, though nearly so - surely it was natural for me to produce a work by a foreigner, a work which had obtained an unprecedented success in Paris, and which, in the result, has been received here with a chorus of enthusiastic praise by the London critics and public.
>
> Whether my permanent English opera scheme is to be realised or not depends now upon the public. The reproach of English opera performances hitherto has been, although good performances have been given and good artists engaged, a lack of completeness in detail and ensemble, an imperfect "production", and an absence of new works. I have shown what can be done and can confidently claim that, in English opera, nothing of equal general all-round excellence in performance, orchestra, chorus, scenery, costumes, ensemble, and stage management has been seen or heard before.

Card Presented to Sir Arthur Sullivan by Members of the Orchestra
On the Occasion of the 100th Performance of *Ivanhoe*
Courtesy of Mr Simon Moss

In starting an enterprise like this many difficulties arise. The prices of admission were at first necessarily high to meet the enormous expenses. It has now, after the experience of a considerable period of working, been found practicable to considerably reduce the expenses of working without in any way impairing the efficiency of the present performance. I have therefore been able to reduce the prices of admission to popular figures, starting upwards (or perhaps I should say downwards) from a gallery at 1s to orchestra stalls at half a guinea - in fact, to absolutely the same prices that are charged at theatres at which small comedy companies are playing.

If the success of *The Basoche* continues long enough I shall no doubt produce from time to time the other works for which I have arranged. I may mention that I have entered into agreements with Mr Goring Thomas, Mr F.H. Cowen, and Mr Hamish McCunn to write new works. Mr Andrew Laing and other authors are writing librettos, and negotiations with other English composers and authors are contemplated. I have secured from Mr Bemberg the right of his new opera (just completed), of which musicians speak in high praise, and I have great satisfaction in stating that Sir Arthur Sullivan has expressed his willingness to write another grand opera later. There will, therefore, be no lack of new works to be produced.

In any other country such an undertaking would not be left to itself, but would be subsidised by the Government of such country as being a valuable help to the advancement of musical art. There is, I imagine, no chance that an English Parliament will do this, and it is not necessary if the public will subsidise it themselves - that is, if they will come in sufficient numbers. The permanent success of the English opera scheme is, therefore, now in the hands of the public; it depends on the public, and the public alone: if they support it and fill the theatre (and the results of *The Basoche* so far seem to promise this) the enterprise can be carried through. (15)

The theatre remained closed for a week, during which the above letter was written. On the day of reopening, Saturday 5th December 1891, the *Pall Mall Gazette* - the pioneer of interview journalism - sent a reporter to see Carte in his office at the Savoy, then playing *The Nautch Girl* by George Dance and Edward Solomon. Carte's *viva voce* comments are altogether more revealing than the bland public relations exercise of his *Times* letter:

It was in Mr Carte's sanctum - not in the spacious boudoir that does duty for the manager's private room - at the Savoy Theatre that Mr D'Oyly Carte received me yesterday (writes our representative). We wanted a talk about the Royal English Opera, which enters on a new lease of life tonight. Of course, I wanted to know what Mr Carte had actually lost by the production of *Ivanhoe*, but ignoring the temporary fall in the banking account under this head, Mr Carte feels that the losses on *Ivanhoe* have been merely so much capital invested in scenery and costumes for one thing, but in very useful experience for another.

"Why." said Mr Carte. "the expenses were very heavy, and just to give you an idea of the magnificence of that production, there were some three thousand hand properties employed in *Ivanhoe*, and ten (*sic*) scenes, as compared with five hundred hand properties and three scenes in *La Basoche*. And yet with it all there has never been the same amount of money taken during a three months' run of a single opera as passed into the treasury during that period after the opening of the Royal English Opera House. Hitherto the best theatre record had been at the Savoy during a part of the run of *The Mikado*. But my expenses with *Ivanhoe* were so very heavy that it was absolutely necessary that this business should continue through the "run" for me to keep open. I had to regulate the charges I made for seats in the theatre by the cost of the production. After a while I found that the artistic public which could afford to pay opera prices was by no means inexhaustible, and my audiences dropped below the paying point. The general public for the cheap parts did not apparently like paying 3s 6d for the pit and 2s for the gallery, and I was playing at a loss. I continued to play the opera up till the vacation, however, and it was my intention upon reopening to give *Ivanhoe* twice a week with *La Basoche* on the other nights. Even with M. Messager's opera as great a success as it ultimately proved to be, I did not receive enough support on the other nights to pay the very heavy sum of money that the salaries of the two companies represented. There were practical difficulties in the way also. It took twelve hours of work by a very large staff to "strike" *Ivanhoe* and mount *La Basoche*, and, of course, that was very difficult to get over. (16) I shall keep operas in readiness - in fact I have plenty in view - but in order to repay the cost of presenting them properly they must be of such a character as will enjoy a "run". The public, too, take some time to discover that an opera is produced." - "And a little longer to find out that it is worth going to, Mr Carte," I interjected.

"Certainly. It took some time for the public to find out that I had reopened the Royal English Opera House a month ago, and after I had resumed quite a fortnight. I met people who asked me when I was going to reopen. Yet when the public got to know of *La Basoche* they came in increasing numbers, and last Saturday [*28 November*] we played to as fine a house as I could wish to see." - "The difficulties of the past swept away, what are you going to do about the future?"

"I shall not think of giving British versions of well-worn operas, but my Royal English Opera House will be devoted to playing opera - for there is no nationality in art - in English. I cannot be expected to carry the idea of everything English to its logical conclusion. English composers - no Irish, or Welsh, or Scotchmen need apply - English singers only, scenes laid in England - why, the thing is ridiculous. A good performance of good opera of the best composers of all countries, sung by artists of all nationalities that can speak English, that is my platform, as the vestreymen used to say, and it only rests with the English. Irish, Welsh and American public to come and support me, and we have a real Royal English Opera. Take Shakespeare's plays. They belong to our national art, I think, and no-one dreams of considering them un-English because the scenes are laid in Venice, in Denmark, in Italy, or in Fairyland, or because Miss Ada Rehan is the Rosalind."

"And your company. Do you intend to form a stock company on the principle of the continental opera houses?" - "This is not a great difficulty, I think. I can give a succession of operas with that perfection of ensemble that makes the Opéra Comique company in Paris so attractive, and I hope by degrees to form a school of English opera singers. What chance have they had in the past? Nothing between light opera and grand opera for a few weeks in the year. The English artist that wishes to go into opera can go round the provinces with the Carl Rosa company, or go to Italy at a salary of nothing at all, or to France for just a little more. Their only chance here is to appear half a dozen times during a short season of two or three months out of the twelve. There has previously been no mart in England for native singers who have a taste and aptitude for serious opera - with an occasional touch of comedy, that is. But I have got together what I think you will agree with me is a good company, and I have no fear for the future. The difficulty has been to induce them to choose between the operatic stage and the concert platform; but experience is everything, and I think we shall be able to engage the artists we want permanently at a yearly remuneration not exceeding the salary of a Cabinet Minister." (17)

Only in our own time, with the establishment of English National Opera at the Coliseum, has Carte's plan for a standing repertory opera company been brought to fruition. However, the company at the Coliseum is maintained by a large government subsidy, without which it would disappear overnight. If such is the state of affairs in modern, supposedly opera-conscious Britain, there need be no surprise at the financial difficulties encountered by Carte. *Ivanhoe*, it seems, took more money in the first three months of its run than *The Mikado*. This is extraordinary. More extraordinary still is the admission that once the box office takings ceased to be greater than those of *The Mikado* the production became financially unsustainable. By this token any of the Gilbert and Sullivan operas would have become unprofitable once the first flush of public enthusiasm was over. Putting the same idea another way we may estimate that the new opera house needed to attract about 1200 people to every performance in order to take as much money (£350) as the Savoy (*Mikado*) when full. Taken over his planned season of six months and 155 performances, this means that the financial viability of Carte's scheme required *Ivanhoe* to attract a total of at least 186,000 people and a sum of £54,250 - in a city and nation whose indifference had always made the production of opera a dubious business. With or without hindsight it is obvious that such a project must fail, and that *Ivanhoe* was the victim of an astonishing act of managerial overconfidence. On the other hand it was done properly and professionally in every respect, perhaps the first English opera ever to be so treated. If his expenditure in such a cause brought about his downfall, Carte's adherence to high standards should always be set down to him as a mark of honour.

It is hard to say whether the week's closure of *La Basoche* affected its subsequent performance at the box office. Certainly the opening flourish that defeated *Ivanhoe* was not sustained when the theatre reopened on Saturday 5th December 1891. Having been given 16 performances up to the break, *La Basoche* survived for a further 43 before closing on 16th January 1892. It is a good work, very Gallic, very accomplished, very refined - sometimes exquisite: but it is for connoisseurs of the French style, not for the huge popular audiences required to sustain the Royal English Opera House. On the same day, 16th January, *The Nautch Girl* came off at the Savoy, leaving Carte temporarily with no opera whatsoever. He could, if he had wished, have produced either *Signa* or *Elaine*, or both, but evidently he had lost the will to fight. The following comment of the *Pall Mall Gazette* is of more than passing significance:

> The question, then, uppermost is whether Londoners really want English opera at all. It is even doubtful whether they want any opera badly. In spite of semi-official notifications to the contrary, we must beg to doubt whether Grand Opera at Covent Garden during the past two or three seasons has been a very great success. If we as a nation have any musical taste, it is apparently all expended on appreciation of oratorio with here and there a belief in the attractiveness of a concert scheme. For opera, however, there is apparently an all-but poverty-stricken audience, a magnificent free list, and poor takings which will not sustain the outgoings on an operatic treasury day. It can hardly be urged that the cause of the failure of Mr Carte's late venture is to be found in the locality of the theatre, for Covent Garden in no less inaccessible, and crowded houses can be occasionally secured there when the quality of the entertainment is of an attractive sort. Here, however, is the rub. *La Basoche* is a most musical opera - an artistic success - but the libretto is of the poorest. Playgoers there are in plenty, and the majority of them do not know a B flat from a bull's foot, and if you are going to attract them into an opera house it is obvious that you must give them something more than music. It is a sad reflection, but one which is forced upon us when we contemplate our only Royal English Opera House given over to the rats and mice. Mr D'Oyly Carte is to be pitied, and it is hard to see how he can continue to throw his operatic pearls before those who do not value them. After all, the Englishman's opera-house is the music-hall. (18)

Unsophisticated audiences were not confined to Shaftesbury Avenue. *Carmen*, now among the most popular of all operas, was restricted to 48 performances on first production in 1875 because the Parisian public found it too demanding. 'The ruminating bourgeois, pot-bellied and ugly, sits in his narrow stall, regretting separation from his kind: he half opens a glassy eye, munches a bonbon, then sleeps again, thinking the orchestra is a-tuning.' These insulting phrases came from Saint-Saens in defence of *Carmen*. Neither Carte nor Sullivan would have been quite so rude about the people who provided their livelihood, but we may speculate that Sullivan provided no overture for *Ivanhoe* because he knew it would not be heard through the conversation of the audience. He certainly abandoned his sombre ending and made cuts in deference to audience taste, real or supposed.

In spite of hopeful press talk of new productions the Royal English Opera House did not reopen. After six months Carte sold the building to Sir Augustus Harris, a theatrical promoter with many irons in the fire:

> According to the *London Figaro* the English Opera House scheme, of which Sir A. Harris will be managing director, is progressing. It is proposed to convert the house into a high-class variety theatre, the purchase price being £255,000 - ie £115.000 in cash. £55.000 in shares, and £85,000 to be left on mortgage. (19)

The figures quoted for the sale are interesting, assuming they are accurate. If we accept Carte's own statement that he had expended 'upwards of £75,000' on the new theatre, (20) add it to the £25,000 allegedly lost on *Ivanhoe*, and deduct the total from the £255,000 paid by Harris for the theatre, we find a difference of about £150,000; If we then treat the first run of *Ivanhoe* as a dead loss and deduct a further £100,000, we are still left with a difference of £50,000. The figures are very rough, but it is difficult to believe that so large a sum could have been entirely absorbed by expenses. Indeed it looks as though Carte may have come out of the affair considerably better off than the defenestrated singers of *Ivanhoe*.

Sullivan's view of these events is best inferred from a comment of B.W. Findon, who was married to one of his, Sullivan's, cousins. 'It is a very suggestive fact', says Findon. 'that in Mr Lawrence's Life Story of Sullivan no mention is made of *Ivanhoe* except in that section of the work which was entrusted to me.' (21) Lawrence's biography was published in the composer's lifetime, and with his co-operation. The omission of all reference to *Ivanhoe* therefore implies an experience too traumatic to be mentioned. Such a reaction seems inappropriate to the actual achievement of *Ivanhoe* in keeping the opera house open for six months. Since, as we learn, it also took more money than *The Mikado* for three of those months, it seems the source of anguish must have lain in the six badly attended performances of November, and Carte's ruthless response to them. Once the singers were dismissed there was no hope of revival. Sullivan will have seen the logic, even the necessity of Carte's action; but something in Carte's decisions, or the way he made them, evidently affected Sullivan deeply, adding insult to the general sense of injury experienced in the trampling of a dream.

NOTES

1) Sullivan & Flower: *Sir Arthur Sullivan*, p. 205.

2) See: Eden, David, *The Cobbler And His Last*, in Sir Arthur Sullivan Society Magazine, No 62, Summer 2006, pp.15-18.

3) Letter from Carte to Sullivan printed in Jacobs: *Arthur Sullivan*, p.270.

4) Letter from Gilbert to Sullivan printed in Jacobs: *Arthur Sullivan*, p.270.

5) *Musical World*: 'King Arthur of the Table Round', 24 Jan 1885.

6) Irving: *Henry Irving*, p. 506.

7) *The Era*, 1 August 1891.

8) *Musical Standard*, 17 January 1885.

9) *Pall Mall Gazette*, 5 April 1892.

10) *Pall Mall Gazette*, 20 March 1891.

11) Margaret Macintyre found Rebecca's music 'very trying': *Pall Mall Gazette*, 5 September 1891.

12) Young: *Sir Arthur Sullivan*, p. 190.

13) *Musical News*, 13 November 1891.

14) Wood: *My Life of Music*, p.43.

15) *The Times*, 3 December 1891.

16) B.W. Findon, in a passage that appears only in the first edition of his work, says that the Royal English Opera House was unfit for its purpose. There was room in the roof only for the scenery of one opera at a time - presumably because the theatre had been intended for the long runs of Gilbert & Sullivan opera. Findon: *Sir Arthur Sullivan*, pp. 140/2. *The Athenaeum* (7 February 1891 p.193) comments on the inadequate number of boxes for wealthy patrons and the small size of the foyer while commending the clear lines of sight in the auditorium.

17) *Pall Mall Gazette*, 5 December 1891.

18) *Pall Mall Gazette*, 16 January 1892.

19) *Musical News*, 15 July 1892. The theatre was finally sold on 28 November 1892.

20) Carte gave this sum in an affidavit of 3rd September 1890 made in the course of the Carpet Quarrel.

21) Findon, *Sir Arthur Sullivan*, p. 135.

BIBLIOGRAPHY

Findon, B.W.: *Sir Arthur Sullivan*, (1st Edition) London, James Nisbet & Co., 1904.

Irving Laurence: *Henry Irving*, London, Faber & Faber, 1951.

Jacobs, Arthur: *Arthur Sullivan, A Victorian Musician*, (2nd Edition), Oxford, Scolar Press, 1992.

Sullivan, Herbert, and Flower, Newman: *Sir Arthur Sullivan*, (2nd Edition) London, Cassell, 1950.

Wood, Henry: *My Life of Music*, London, Gollancz, 1938.

EUGÈNE OUDIN
AS THE TEMPLAR

IVANHOE – THREE REVIEWS

At last the day has come! Our foremost composer – foremost by right of the marvellous versatility by which he has always been able to appeal to the ears of both his learned and his unlearned hearers – has found the opportunity which he has probably desired as ardently as his keenest admirers, and has added a serious romantic opera to the list of his musical achievements. It is what we have all hoped for, even demanded, for many a long year past; and now that our wishes have been fulfilled we cannot choose but congratulate ourselves on the brightened prospects of the English lyric stage. That Sir Arthur Sullivan has completely succeeded cannot be doubted for a moment. As a consummate tune-writer we have known him for long. The records of the Savoy Theatre, and, still further back, the Opéra Comique, bear witness to his powers as a creator of captivating melody. On the other hand, we have not wanted evidence of his ability to deal with more dramatic material. Those magnificent cantatas *The Martyr of Antioch* and *The Golden Legend* told us what to expect when Sir Arthur finally made up his mind to come forward as a composer of grand opera. *Ivanhoe*, let us say at once, combines the melodic and dramatic elements in beautiful proportion. In some quarters there may possibly be complaints at Sir Arthur's refusal to swear complete allegiance to the "advanced school." There will doubtless be some little carping at the simplicity and straightforwardness of many of his themes and much of his treatment. But these views will certainly not prevail with the vast majority of music lovers. In our opinion the composer of *Ivanhoe* has struck a most happy medium between the set forms of the past and the rhapsodical diffuseness of extreme Wagnerism; and, if we mistake not, his medium will be a genuinely popular one in the ears of all.

Pall Mall Gazette, 2 February 1891, p.1-2.

As a work of art Sir Arthur Sullivan's first grand opera has been variously criticised, according to the different standpoints of the writers, some of whom have unquestionably erred in the direction of panegyric, while others have shown bias and prejudice against the work to an extent as discreditable as it is silly. The truth lies between the two extremes, the composer having succeeded as well as it was likely he would succeed, having regard to the direction in which his genius has been previously engaged. The purely lyrical portions of the score are truly admirable, and those who still cherish a fondness for rhythmical melody will find as much that is frank and fresh as can reasonably be desired. We referred last week [*7 February, p.194*] to the frequently interesting nature of the accompaniments, and have only to add that the composer shows himself a master in his treatment of the orchestra, though the scoring is more remarkable for Schubertian delicacy than Wagnerian fullness and sonority. Another feature of the score to which we drew attention has been made the ground of much adverse criticism, namely the extreme simplicity of the vocal part-writing. It must be confessed that from the musician's standpoint this is a weakness such as one does not expect to find in a modern grand opera. Wherever concerted music occurs, either with or without chorus, it is singularly unpretentious, even when in harmony, while the frequent employment of unison, however effective it may seem to ordinary listeners, certainly gives a suggestion of vulgarity to those of more cultivated tastes. It would almost seem as if Sir Arthur Sullivan had taken the capacities of provincial companies into account when composing the opera. It is certain that in the German cities, where *Ivanhoe* is to be produced in due course, those who can find no merit in English music will be quick to perceive this unquestionable defect. That the declamatory music is, on the whole, rather poor and wanting in dramatic force may also be admitted, and here we have said the last that can be said in the way of disparagement. On the other hand the melodic beauty in which it abounds, the fresh, breezy style in which every episode is handled, and the absolute freedom from all suspicion of labour in construction, are positive merits rarely to be met with in an operatic score of the present day, and are sufficient to justify impartial critics in pronouncing the work on the whole a startling success, and in predicting for it a lengthy career of popularity among all classes of music lovers.

Athenaeum 14 February 1891, p.226.

. . . . Coming to the music, it is evident that certain good features were assured beforehand. It was perfectly well- known that Sir Arthur Sullivan would write an orchestral score full of charm, in which the genius of each instrument would be carefully studied, and every resource turned to musicianly account, in the style of the greatest masters of the art. In modern opera, even as here modified, this is a most important advantage, appreciable not only by the connoisseur who knows why he is gratified, but by the many who are gratified and don't know why. The orchestral score has, further, the now rare merit of keeping in its proper place and discharging its rightful function of attending upon and ministering to the effect of the voices. While the stage-song continues the orchestra does not dispute its pre-eminence or divide interest and attention by starting along an independent line. In other words, it is "symphonic," in the Wagnerian sense, only when working alone. It uses recurring themes sparingly, and that is another advantage. Being so few the subjects are readily identified, and their significance understood whenever they appear. "Leading themes" they can hardly be called. The vocal music is perfectly characteristic of the composer. Everybody familiar with *The Golden Legend* knows the stamp of it, and can recognise as Sullivanesque the easy, flowing tune, refined, yet adapted to popularity; the instinctive at any rate, unlaboured — fitting of melody to the spirit of the words, so that the poet's thought and its musical expression seem exactly to suit each other; and the all-pervading sense of beauty, of which this composer never loses sight, even when dealing with sentiments and situations that painfully jar upon feeling. But the *Ivanhoe* music makes a revelation which adds materially to our knowledge of the composer and raises him to a higher level than, in public consciousness, he has ever before occupied. All Sir Arthur Sullivan's works earlier than *Ivanhoe* had left in doubt the important point whether he could deal adequately with a strong dramatic situation. Neither the *Martyr of Antioch* nor *The Golden Legend* had given satisfactory evidence upon this point, and the whole matter was in suspense till the first performance of *Ivanhoe* set it at rest. Doubt is possible no longer, if only because we have heard the masterly and exciting duet for Rebecca and the Templar - one of those operatic numbers that leave their mark on all who hear them. Here the level of a fine and strenuous situation is easily reached by the musician, nor are there wanting other examples, albeit the opportunities afforded by the last scene of the final act were not fully utilised by the wearied and time-pressed composer. We do not understand why Sir Arthur avoided that fine operatic means, a fully developed *ensemble*; but he has chosen to do so, and put his strength into the lyrics, which, it may be, the public most appreciate. These are of many kinds and varied merit, two standing out conspicuously — the "Sleep" song of Ivanhoe and Friar Tuck's "Ho, jolly Jenkin!" than which, in its way, nothing could be happier. Our space is nearly exhausted and our remarks must draw to a close, with congratulations addressed to all who had part in the production of a work destined to exercise great influence upon the future course of English opera.

Musical Times 1 March 1891, p.150.

THE END OF THE AFFAIR – THE PALACE THEATRE OF VARIETIES

15

JULIAN STURGIS 1848-1904

Courtesy of Miranda Seymour

JULIAN RUSSELL STURGIS 1848-1904

By David Eden

Approaching Julian Sturgis from the perspective of his work with Sullivan we see him as the librettist of *Ivanhoe*, and nothing else. He seems a shadowy figure, even more obscure than Basil Hood, the librettist of *The Rose of Persia*. To see him in his habit as he lived we must turn to the merchant aristocracy of Boston in the eighteenth and nineteenth centuries. In Boston the names Russell and Sturgis are still familiar as part of the network of wealthy families who used to dominate the town.

The first Sturgis who concerns us is Russell Sturgis (1750-1826), a trader in hats and furs who married Elizabeth Perkins of Cape Cod (1756-1843). He served in the miltia, represented Boston in the Massachusetts State Senate in 1801, and in 1805 stood unsuccessfully as a Republican Senator. He also expanded his horizons as a trader. His brothers-in-law, James Perkins (1761-1822) and Thomas Handasyd Perkins (1765-1854) traded along the Northwest Coast and with China as the firm of J. & T. H. Perkins. In 1795 Sturgis joined them and a few others in the ownership of a new ship, the *Grand Turk*, which was sent to Canton in March 1796. When the Perkins' decided to establish a branch office in Canton in 1803, Sturgis invested substantially in the venture. Three of his sons went to China: Henry Sturgis (1790-1819) who died in Macao aged twenty-nine; George Washington Sturgis (1793-1826), who was in Canton between 1810 and 1823; and James Perkins Sturgis (1791-1851) who arrived in Canton in 1809 and died on his voyage home in 1851. In 1818 the three brothers, as partners in the firm of James P. Sturgis and Company, were all involved in the lucrative trade with China, exporting tea and balancing that with the import of opium, the only commodity for which the Chinese seemed to crave. Then as now the tea and drugs trade meant wealth, but in those days opium carried no social stigma, as an obituary of Russell Sturgis reveals:

> Mr. Sturgis was a native of Barnstable [*Massachusetts*] and of an ancient and respectable family. He came to Boston when young. He was a respectable merchant, an honest man, an ardent patriot, and an affectionate friend. His wife was named executrix of his estate. Apart from one thousand dollar bequests to his surviving children, the remainder of his estate was given to his wife. Although no inventory was filed at the time of his death, one was completed after Elizabeth Perkins Sturgis died on September 8, 1843. At that time her real estate was valued at ten thousand dollars and her personal estate at more than thirty-seven thousand dollars. (1)

The Sturgises had 16 children in all, most of whom died in infancy. Only one son, Nathaniel Russell Sturgis (1779-1856), actually had children of his own. His son, also christened Nathaniel made life difficult by calling himself plain Russell Sturgis and added to the complications by marrying three times.

Russell Sturgis (1805-1887) was a substantial figure in the history of Boston. He was born in Boston, went to Harvard at the age of twelve, and in 1828, immediately after the death of his first wife, made his first voyage to Europe, where he met his future second wife. He settled in Boston as a lawyer and would probably have continued in this profession had he not overheard his relation John. P. Cushing speak of the unwillingness of a certain person to go to China. 'I wish I had that chance offered me,' remarked Sturgis. In a few days the opportunity was given to him and he sailed for Canton in 1833. He entered the firm of Russell & Sturgis of Manila, and was a founder partner of Russell, Sturgis & Co. of Canton, in 1833. In 1840, after the crash of 1837 and the bankruptcy of the Canton firm, the house consolidated with Russell & Co. Two years later Russell Sturgis became a partner. We know something of his life in Canton because his son Julian - our Julian - published a memoir of him in 1894. It seems that the East had a great fascination for him, and in fact for all the men who went out there from Boston. The life there was new and interesting to them, and they assumed great responsibilities. They lived a life of considerable freedom, although they were not allowed to go outside the Factory reservation. Besides being called foreign devils they were also described as 'a ghostly tribe of barbarians,' as 'uncouth beings with fiery hair,' as 'a strange people who came to the Flowery Kingdom from regions of mist and storm where the sun never shines,' and finally as 'wild, untamed men whose words are rough, and whose language is confused.'

In 1844 Russell Sturgis retired from business in the East and came home to Boston to join his children, who had been sent there to school - their mother, his second wife, Mary Greene Hubbard, had died in Manila on 17 Sep 1837 shortly after the birth of her fourth child, Mary Greene Sturgis (18 Jun 1837 - 28 Apr 1838). On 2 Nov 1846 he married Julia Overing Boit (1827-1888), having three sons and a daughter:

> 1) Henry Parkman Sturgis, (1847-1933) who became a Liberal M.P. and married first Polly (Margaret) Brand, the daughter of Lord Hampden. After her death in 1886 he married secondly, in 1894, Marie Eveleen, the daughter of George Meredith by his marriage to Marie Vulliamy. (2)

> 2) Julian Russell Sturgis. Born 21 October 1848. Died 13 April 1904. Married 8 November 1883 Mary Maud Beresford, daughter of Colonel M.W.D. Beresford, who was born in Barbados in 1858 and died 30 April 1952. They had three children - Mark Beresford Russell Sturgis (born 1884); Gerard Boit Sturgis (born 1885), and Roland Josslyn Sturgis (1888-1980).

> 3) Mary Greene Hubbard Sturgis, b. 2 Feb 1851; m. 1st Leopold Richard Seymour 5 Jul 1871; 2nd. Bertram Godfrey Falle, later Lord Portsea, 18 Jul 1906.

> 4) Howard Overing Sturgis (1855-1920). Unmarried. (3)

The newly married Russell Sturgis found the scale of living at home in Boston more expensive than he had expected, and in 1849 he was faced with the choice of joining Russell & Co in China, or joining Barings Bank in London, where Joshua Bates, the husband of his cousin Lucretia Sturgis, was a senior partner. He chose to accompany Joshua Bates to London, and in due course became a partner in Barings, finally becoming head of the house. (4) In fact, he stayed in England for the rest of his life, dying here on 2 November 1887.

One outcome of the family move to England was that the Sturgis children became effectively English rather than American. We speak of Julian as American because he was born in Boston, but in fact he lived in England from the age of a few months. He went to Eton and Balliol, where he rowed for three years in the college eight. (5) He also played football, because he played for the Wanderers, who beat Oxford University 2 - 0 in the Cup Final of 1873. This was only the second Cup Final ever played, the Wanderers having won the first against the Royal Engineers in 1872. In those days professional football as we know it did not exist, and the leading teams were made up of gentlemen amateurs like Sturgis. He must have played football both at Eton and Oxford because the Wanderers was a team made up of former public school and varsity men. In fact the Wanderers won the cup 5 times before the professionals began to oust the amateurs. Owing no doubt to their effortless superiority the Old Etonians were also a force to be reckoned with. They appeared in 6 cup finals, winning 2 and losing 4. In the 1876 final Julian Sturgis was a member of the Old Etonians team when they lost 3 - 0 to Wanderers. The match was played at Kennington Oval, having gone to a replay after a 1 - 1 draw, which the Old Etonians would have won if a goal post had not collapsed.

Julian Sturgis did not play in another cup final, but he scored 3 against Minerva in the third round in 1878/9, when Old Etonians went on to beat Clapham 1 - 0 in the final. There is nothing to indicate why he was not in the team, but he had recently returned from a trip to the Levant, where he visited the Turkish and Russian armies before Constantinople. He had become a barrister of the Inner Temple in 1876, though it is not clear whether he actually practised. In 1880 he spent nine months in America at Leadville, Colorado, in the Rocky Mountains. (6) The implication is that he had gone silver mining, because Leadville is the place where the Unsinkable Molly Brown's husband struck it rich.

In those days barristers often turned to literature as a way of passing the time and making ends meet. Coming from such a wealthy background Sturgis had no need of money, but he had 'displayed marked literary ability' while at Oxford. His first published story, *John-A-Dreams* (1878), 'received from the critics and the general public a full meed of approbation.' (7)   In 1879 he published a novel called *An Accomplished Gentleman*, followed in 1882 by *Dick's Wandering*. In 1889 came a novel called *Comedy of a Country House*. *The Spectator* gave it a cautiously good review:

> Mr Sturgis is a very clever man, and there is so much cleverness in his *Comedy of a Country House* that no reader who knows good work when he sees it, can fail to render hearty and ungrudging admiration. . . . . The true tone of comedy is, on the whole, admirably maintained. (8)

In the meantime we may record Julian Sturgis' first operatic venture, which was the libretto for Arthur Goring Thomas's *Nadeshda*, produced by the Carl Rosa Company at Drury Lane on 16 April 1885, that is a month after *The Mikado*. Thomas, a pupil of Sullivan, had previously had a great success with *Esmeralda*, coinciding in this case with the run of *Iolanthe*. *Nadeshda* did not achieve quite the same success as *Esmeralda*, but it was well received, and it obviously laid the foundation of Sturgis' reputation as a librettist. This is what *The Times* had to say - presumably the writer is the paper's music critic, Francis Hueffer:

> The libretto by Mr Julian Sturgis is founded upon a Russian story more immediately derived from a German source. . . . . There is, as a matter of fact, a German novel dealing with the same or a similar subject, which, however, not having read, we cannot speak of. Wherever or in what shape Mr Sturgis may have found his materials, he has treated them

JULIAN STURGIS

Courtesy of Mr Tim Sturgis

in a clever and workmanlike manner. His diction is not very refined or elevated, and his metre in rhymed lyrics or blank verse often defies the rules of prosody. But the incidents of the story are set forth simply and clearly, and more than one powerful situation is attained. Altogether his work shows a welcome change from the lines laid down by the "poet Bunn" and the late Mr Fitzball, which old-fashioned critics still believe to be the most congenial medium for English music. (9)

Like *Ivanhoe*, *Nadeshda* was described as a 'romantic opera'. It was thorough-composed, and Sturgis' contribution seems to have been to make a departure from the traditional English opera libretto by creating what we would call an organic fusion between the set-piece arias and the narrative or dramatic part of the text. It is reasonable to conclude that Sullivan must have known Sturgis before they began to work together in 1890/1 - they might well have been introduced by Goring Thomas at the première of *Nadeshda*. Bernard Shaw took the characteristically flippant view that Sullivan deserved the libretto of *Ivanhoe* as a punishment for not writing it himself. It would be nearer the truth to say that Sullivan had a clear idea of what he wanted, and Sturgis proved a congenial collaborator - 'He is quick at seizing my meaning, and falls into it with kindly readiness', as Sullivan put it. (10) In this sense Sullivan did indeed write the libretto himself. Left to his own devices Sturgis might have preferred to concentrate on the love stories of the novel in order to produce an organically worked-out plot, but at the behest of Sullivan he produced a précis or epitome of the whole novel - the musical of the book, so to speak. At the same time he employed the methods he had already used in *Nadeshda* to embed the songs dramatically within the narrative.

Sturgis did not write another libretto until 1901, when he provided Stanford with *Much Ado About Nothing*. (11) He did however write several books, including two novels called *The Folly of Pen Harrington* (1897) and *Stephen Calinari* (1901). Hubert Parry set a number of his lyrics in the various sets of his *English Lyrics*. It seems that Sturgis first met Parry at Eton. Finally he wrote the libretto of *The Cricket on the Hearth* for Alexander Mackenzie, though this was not produced until 1914, ten years after his death. (12)

There is not much to be said about Sturgis personally. In 1896 he commissioned a new house at Hogs Back near Guildford from the architect Charles Francis Voysey (1857-1941). This house, variously known as Sturgis House, Wancote or Greyfriars, is regarded by architectural historians as an outstanding example of the arts and crafts style. It tells us something about Sturgis' taste, and the money he had at his disposal.

Julian Sturgis died on 13 April 1904, not at Hogs Back but at 16 Hans Road, London S.W. He was however buried close to the Hogs Back, in the graveyard of the Watts Chapel, Compton, near Guildford, and has a charming Arts and Crafts grave there. The *Times* obituary informs us that he was a member of the Athenaeum, White's, and St James's clubs, which unfortunately tells us very little. His wife, whose nickname was Pussy, lived to the age of 94, dying in 1952.

The eldest son of the marriage was Mark, or rather Sir Mark Beresford Sturgis, who died in 1949 as a KCB. He spent a most of his career in Ireland as an administrator, and was a Fellow of the Eugenics Society. In 1914 he married Lady Rachel Montagu Stuart Wortley.

The second son, Gerard Boit Sturgis, died when he was comparatively young and is buried close to his father, with a tablet in the adjoining cloister. The third son, Roland Josslyn Russell Sturgis, married the actress Christine Silver (1883-1960) in 1918 after the death of her first husband, Walter Hamilton Maxwell. His great delight was to drive a horse and carriage along the beach in Boulogne, not being able to find anywhere in England suitable for the purpose. (13) Christine Silver had a prominent career on the stage. She also made films, beginning in 1917 with *Chicken Casey*, and ending in 1955 with *The Hornet's Nest*.

Julian Sturgis was not at home on Census night in 1901.(14) Instead we find him at a place called Queen's Acre, his brother Howard's home on the edge of Windsor Great Park. He is there with his wife, Mary, and several other people including Henry James, that is to say *the* Henry James, the novelist, whom he first met in 1877. This carries us unexpectedly into the social world of Henry James, and introduces us to Julian's brother Howard, nicknamed Howdie, who was one of James's greatest friends.

For obvious reasons Howard Sturgis shared his brother's background. He went to Eton, and Trinity College Cambridge, taking his BA in 1878. He also wrote novels, and was a great social entertainer:

> Whom did he entertain? Visiting American cousins and acquaintance (who sometimes outstayed their welcome) and American expatriates such as himself. Most of the guests were lively and literary. There was Henry James, oppressed as ever with his efforts to find the exact phrase to convey the intricate conceptions passing through his mind. There were the fashionable novelists, Edith Wharton and Rhoda Broughton. There were courtiers from Windsor Castle, diplomats *en route* for their embassy, a few dandies, Eton beaks, and occasionally their wives. Blanche Warre-Cornish, wife of the Vice-Provost of Eton and sister of the editor of the *Times Literary Supplement*, was a renowned conversationalist who could be relied upon, as her daughter records in *A Nineteenth Century Childhood*, to keep the company on 'her fine imaginative plateau and expect others to come up and join her there.' Sitting among his guests, the golden-haired Howdie — in later years his hair turned to silver — might sew, or knit, but more often he would retire behind an embroidery frame with a basket of bright silks beside him, plunging the needle through, pulling it out at the back and then guiding it to re-emerge at the front. He would watch the conversation, giving a little nudge if it began to flag and then withdraw to let others shine. But by nature he was an indefatigable talker. (15)

Another of Howard's friends was the novelist Edith Wharton. In her autobiography *A Backward Glance* Edith Wharton gives a lengthy description of Sturgis and his house, nicknamed Qu'acre, from which it becomes clear that everyone accepted him as he was:

> A long low drawing-room; white-panelled walls hung with water-colours of varying merit; curtains and furniture of faded slippery chintz; French windows opening on a crazy wooden verandah, through which, on one side, one caught a glimpse of a weedy lawn and a shrubbery edged with an unsuccessful herbaceous border, on the other, of a not too successful rose garden, with a dancing faun poised above an incongruously "arty" blue-tiled pool. Within, profound chintz arm-chairs drawn up about a hearth on which a fire always smouldered; a big table piled with popular novels and picture-magazines; and near the table a lounge on which lay outstretched, his legs covered by a thick shawl, his hands occupied with knitting-needles or embroidery silks, a sturdily-built handsome man with brilliantly white wavy hair, a girlishly clear complexion, a black moustache, and tender mocking eyes under the bold arch of his black brows. (16)

There is no space here to quote Edith Wharton's account in full - she seems to say that Howard used to walk into Eton in a bonnet and shawl. What she does not say is that many of the visitors were young men for whom Howdie picked flowers, and that he had once fallen for Percy Lubbock, his House Captain at Eton. He was also a friend of A.C. Ainger, his former housemaster, who is remembered as the author of the Eton school song. The two rented a house in Wales, to which they invited the boys. (17)

Also present on census night was Howard's cousin, William Haynes Smith, known as the Babe, who was a fixture in his life. Smith was actually a hearty type who read *The Pink 'Un* rather than *The Golden Bowl*; he was a member of the Stock Exchange, looking after Howard's investments with very poor results. (18)   Some of Howard's friends, including Henry James, were mistrustful of his power. It seems possible that Howard saw Smith as possessing the qualities in which he was deficient himself. After Howard's death in 1920 Smith married one of his, Howard's, American cousins, Maud Sturgis.

Howard Sturgis wrote two novels, *Tim* (1891) and *Belchamber* (1904). They were considered rather better than his brother's, and *Belchamber* is now regarded as a minor classic, though Howard was mortified by James' mild circumlocutory comments. (19) Both books belong to the underground 'gay' literature of the time, though *Belchamber* is the more substantial of the two. (20) It concerns the life of a quiet boy, a misfit, who is exploited by his extroverted and athletic younger brother. Whether this is code for Howard's relationship with Julian is not apparent, but it seems likely enough.

CHRISTINE SILVER (FAR RIGHT) WITH LAURENCE GROSSMITH

In *An Englishman's Home* (Wyndham's Theatre, 27 Jan 1909)

23

ALL DICKY WITH IVANHOE; or, THE LONG AND SHORT OF IT

Julian Sturgis with Arthur Sullivan

Punch, 14 February 1891

NOTES

This essay is a revised version of a talk given at the Sir Arthur Sullivan Society Festival, Cirencester Agricultural College, 1 October 2005. Except where specific sources are cited, the information has been taken from internet sites concerning the Sturgis family of Boston and the FA Cup. Caveat emptor.

1) Online source, *Captains of Boston*, quoting the *Boston Commercial Gazette*.

2) Williams, *George Meredith*, p.189 ff.

3) *Times* obituary of Howard Sturgis 10 Feb 1920; will: 8 Apr 1920.

4) I am indebted for this account to Mr Tim Sturgis, based on current research in the archives of the Massachusetts Historical Society, Boston, and Ing Barings, London. It differs from the story told by Julian Sturgis in his biography of his father, which includes more corroborative detail than the facts appear to warrant.

5) *Daily Telegraph* obituary of Julian Sturgis, 15 April 1904, p.10.

6) *Times* obituary of Julian Sturgis,14 April 1904 p.5.

7) *Daily Telegraph* obituary of Julian Sturgis, 15 April 1904, p.10.

8) *Spectator*, 27 July 1887, p.116.

9) *Times* 16 April 1885, p.8.

10) Sullivan & Flower: p.205.

11) *Much Ado About Nothing*: Covent Garden, 30 May 1901. Some say that this is an opera Sullivan should have written instead of *Ivanhoe*. We may at least agree that it is an opera Sullivan should have written instead of Stanford.

12) *The Cricket on the Hearth*: Royal Academy of Music, 6 June 1914.

13) Personal communication from Mr Tim Sturgis.

14) 1901 Census: New Windsor, Berks, Parish of St John the Baptist; RG13/1168.

15) Annan, Noel, *in*: Sturgis, *Belchamber*, Introduction, pp. v-vi.

16) Wharton, *A Backward Glance*, p.225. Further information is added by the *Times* obituary of Howard Sturgis, 10 Feb 1920, p.15.

17) *Times* obituary of A.C. Ainger, 29 Oct 1919.

18) Personal communication from Mr Tim Sturgis.

19) Annan, Noel, *in*: Sturgis, *Belchamber*, Introduction, p. xii.

20) In the view of Mr Tim Sturgis *Belchamber* is too wide ranging and significant to be considered merely 'gay.' (Personal communication.)

BIBLIOGRAPHY

Pike, William Thomas: *Surrey at the Opening of the Twentieth Century*; W.T.Pike & Co, New Century Series No 24. (Includes a photograph and short biography of Julian Sturgis.)

Sturgis, Howard Overing: *Belchamber*, with an introduction by Noel Annan, O.U.P., 1986.

Sturgis, Julian: *From the Books and Papers of Russell Sturgis*. Edited by his son Julian Sturgis. 1894.

Sullivan, Herbert, and Flower, Newman: *Sir Arthur Sullivan, His Life, Letters and Diaries*, (2nd ed), Cassell, 1950.

Wharton, Edith: *A Backward Glance*; D. Appleton Century Co., 1934.

Williams. David: *George Meredith – His Life and Lost Love*; Hamish Hamilton, 1977.

WORKS OF JULIAN STURGIS

John-a-Dreams. A tale. 1878.
An Accomplished Gentleman. A novel. 1879.
Little Comedies. 1880.
Dick's Wandering. A novel. 1882.
Little Comedies, Old and New. 1882.
A Master of Fortune.
My Friends and I. Three tales. (Ed). 1884.
Nadeshda. Romantic Opera in 4 acts. 1885.
John Maidment, 1885.
Thraldom. A novel. 1887.
Comedy of a Country House. 1889.
Count Julian - A Spanish tragedy. (In verse.) 1893.
Ivanhoe. A romantic opera adapted from Sir Walter Scott's novel. 1891.
After Twenty Years, and other stories, 1892.
From the Books and Papers of Russell Sturgis. Edited by his son, Julian Sturgis. Privately printed, 1894.
A Book of Song. 1894.
The Folly of Pen Harrington. A novel.1897
Much Ado about Nothing. Opera in 4 acts, founded on Shakespeare's comedy. 1901.
Cricket on the Hearth. Founded on Dickens' novel. Opera in 3 acts. 1901.
Stephen Calinari. A novel. 1901
The Prime Minister's Pamphlet - Notes on Insular Free Trade.1903.
Fireflies. Opera with music by J.E. Barkworth. Royal College of Music,1925.

THE MUSICAL TIMES ON THE LIBRETTO

The libretto of *Ivanhoe* is, as all the world knows, the work of Mr. Julian Sturgis, a gentleman whom Americans claim as one of themselves. A previous opera-book, that of *Nadeshda*, had prepared the public for a work of adequate merit; and, on the whole, expectation has not been disappointed. Mr. Sturgis is at his best in the lyrics. He has a pretty knack of versifying, and we may give a few lines as a sample:—

> Fair and lovely is the may,
>
> Blushing 'neath the kiss of day;
>
> Lovelier, fairer blooms the rose,
>
> Dreaming in the garden close;
>
> Fairest, loveliest is the bloom
>
> Of the golden-gloried broom.

Sir Arthur Sullivan's librettist can go on rhyming thus to any extent embodying in musical verse many a pleasant and dainty idea. We like Mr. Sturgis's blank verse much less, even when, as is often the case, it has the merit of appropriate language. Like David in Saul's armour, Mr. Sturgis, in the "heroic measure," is cumbered and not at ease. Moreover, he gives way to considerable irregularity without apparent reason. But it is scarcely justifiable to cavil, seeing how very far superior to the general run is the book of *Ivanhoe* in all that concerns literary quality. We recognise this fact with much pleasure, as another proof that the day of the old libretto, with all that made "Poet Bunn" ridiculous, has passed away. In framing an opera out of Scott's novel, Mr. Sturgis had a difficult task — so much so, that we doubt if he has thoroughly satisfied many of his critics. For ourselves, we hold that the scenes are well-chosen, though some of the incidents are unnecessary to the completeness of the argument. Such is the King's interview with and dismissal of De Bracey in the last act. This has no importance whatever, and should be excised forthwith. As just stated, the scenes are well chosen, but their sequence might be improved and their details revised with advantage. In the duet for Rebecca and the Templar there is an anti-climax after the Jewish girl has threatened to hurl herself from the tower. Why should the situation, having reached its proper crisis, be tamely prolonged? Then the scene of the destruction of Torquilstone Castle is risky and only saved by the fineness of the picture. What force is it that sends the roof of Ivanhoe's chamber skyward? and why, when the walls collapse, is the castle seen burning a long way off? These doubtful points in the staging of the piece do not stand alone, but we must admit, on the other hand, that non-critical eyes are dazzled by a brilliant series of varied pictures, changing frequently from one sort of interest to another, a keeping attention not only alive but alert. All blemishes notwithstanding, the literary and dramatic parts of *Ivanhoe* are a success in a degree for which well-wishers to English opera cannot be sufficiently thankful.

Musical Times, 1ˢᵗ March 1891

MISS PALLISER AS ROWENA IN *IVANHOE*.
(Drawn by Percy Anderson.)

CONTRAST AND UNITY IN THE SCORE OF IVANHOE

By Martin Yates

One of Sullivan's strengths as a composer was his use of contrast as a musical feature. This is especially true of the large-scale works, where it is evident that his desire was to entertain and delight his audience with interesting and varied musical ideas. The contrasts in *The Golden Legend* are achieved through the use of the particular tonal qualities of different instrumental groups; in *Ivanhoe*, where the orchestra plays a less dominant role, contrast is achieved by varying the musical texture – a procedure which is open to misinterpretation, because commentators often speak of differing musical styles being employed and accuse Sullivan of being unsure of his aims. Careful study of the context of such sections shows clearly that each is used as an aid to the dramatic scheme.

These contrasts in the musical texture are achieved through the density of the writing, the timbre of keys, and chromatic and diatonic harmony. Generally the thick textures and abundant chromatic harmony of *The Golden Legend* are avoided in favour of a more 'open', less experimental style. Diatonic harmony is especially employed in the outdoor scenes, where it is combined with use of 'lighter' keys like G-major, D-major and F-major, while chromatic harmony, which allows more harmonic freedom, is reserved chiefly for the intimate scenes such as the duets for Rowena and Ivanhoe (Act I Scene 2), Rebecca and the Templar (II/3) and the Torquilstone scenes generally. Combined with the use of 'dark' keys – Ab-major/minor, Eb-minor, Gb-major – and a thicker orchestral texture, these create a sombre and forbidding atmosphere. However, to avoid giving a disjointed effect Sullivan also employs musical features to unify the opera – between acts, within scenes, and within individual solo or duet numbers. These features may be summarised as the use of motifs, key melodic phrases, a planned key scheme, and particular rhythmic and melodic elements. Throughout the opera, therefore, one sees evidence of the basic compositional aims of *contrast* and *unity* as servants to the dramatic needs of the story. Sullivan's integration of these features produces a score which is remarkably consistent in its own terms.

The Dramatic Structure

As Sullivan himself remarked, one of the problems with the story of *Ivanhoe* was that in order to be faithful to the whole novel, it could not be shortened to anything less than three scenes in each of the three acts. The librettist, Julian Sturgis, planned each act in order to reflect Sullivan's dramatic aims regarding contrast. Act I has an intimate lyrical scene between two of larger dimensions – Rotherwood and the lists at Ashby. Act III has a lyrical outdoor scene between two of more dramatic interest. In the original concept of Act II, the outdoor scene at Copmanhurst was placed between the two scenes at Torquilstone. Problems of stage management probably dictated its move to the beginning of the act, and although this goes against the dramatic scheme originally intended by Sturgis, Sullivan probably saw the *musical* gains of having all the 'dark' Torquilstone scenes together, linked by the key of Gb-major. As this was how the opera was finally performed and published, one must consider that this order of scenes in Act II was what Sullivan wished.

Nevertheless the opera still shows a balance between scenes of dramatic importance and others of respite from the action – the lyrical beauty of the Rowena/Ivanhoe duet, the humour of the King Richard/Friar Tuck exchanges, and the reconciliation of the Glade scene. They are so, to speak, the dainty meats between the bread and butter.

The Key Scheme

The key scheme of the opera is planned by Sullivan both to show unity, by connecting various scenes or episodes within scenes, and contrast, by the use of different keys.

The first scene of the opera, in Rotherwood, begins and ends in C-major, thus enclosing the entire scene with a single key. The second scene – 'An ante-room in Rotherwood' – is linked to the previous one by woodwind chords suggesting C-major. However this quickly turns via A-minor to E-major for Rowena's aria, only to return at the end of the scene to C-minor, thus bringing us back close to the original key. The outburst at the beginning of the Ashby scene is effective not only because of a totally different key (Eb-major) but also because the scoring of the final phases of the previous scene consists of light pizzicato strings. The focal point of the Ashby scene is the chorus 'Plantagenesta!' which is repeated at the end in its original key of G-major.

The scene at Copmanhurst which opens Act II is enclosed within D-major, but the keys chosen for the next two scenes in Torquilstone Castle depict the gloom and claustrophobic atmosphere. Bb-minor begins the second scene, and Gb-major – Brian's aria 'Woo thou thy snowflake' – finishes it. The opening of the final scene is in Eb-minor, but the first four bars suggest the key of the previous scene – Gb-major. Thus Sullivan makes clear the connection between the two scenes. The final scene ends in Ab-major, which is the key of the confrontation duet between Rebecca and the Templar.

The first scene of the final act begins in F-major and ends in E-minor. Desiring a complete contrast for the next (Glade) scene, Sullivan begins in a clear G-major; the final trio of the scene is in D-major, and a sense of connection is achieved with the finale, the opening bars of which suggest D-major. This, however, turns out to be the dominant for the G-major chorus of Templars. The opera ends with a chorus in B-major, which repeats both the music and the key of the quartet in the previous scene.

The use of keys within each scene is of course more complex than the above account suggests. Indeed, Sullivan's use of specific keys for their 'colour' rises to the level of a dramatic device, and it will be seen as this article progresses that keys play a major part in the suggestion of contrast and unity.

Individual 'Numbers'

The use of contrast also extends to the handling of individual numbers, especially the strophic songs, of which there are three in the score. 'Ho, jolly Jenkin' plays through twice without any change – it does not need any! – but in the other two songs Sullivan introduces an orchestral feature in the second verse which was absent in the first, thus attracting the listener's attention immediately. In Rowena's beautifully scored 'O moon art thou clad' the harp is added – its semi-quaver figures suggesting the 'whispering wind'. Indeed this beautiful aria with its pulsing woodwind chords – three flutes and clarinets – intricate string writing and a slowly changing bass line strongly suggests the effects achieved in the operatic music of the American minimalist composer John Adams!

In Rebecca's prayer the cor anglais is a moving addition to the scoring. Even in the non-strophic numbers Sullivan sometimes adds an extra feature – like the harp which perfectly suggests the 'Maid of Judah' trembling in the arms of the Templar ('Woo thou thy snowflake' II/2) or the fluttering woodwind in 'Plantagenesta!' and swirling violins in 'I ask nor wealth'.

The Use of Motifs

Unity in the score is achieved primarily through the use of motifs and key melodic phrases associated not only with specific people but also with ideals and, in one case, with the recurrence of conflict. They are not used in the all-pervading manner of Wagner, but are employed by Sullivan as musical touchstones on the subconscious of his audience in order to link dramatic ideas and situations.

In the whole opera there are only three genuine motifs, which are used in a fairly consistent manner. The first is a 'Norman Knight' motif, which is introduced during Cedric's opening solo at the words 'his knights, his Norman knights'. This is built upon a triadic figure, the first cousin of the 'Tower' motif in *The Yeomen of the Guard*; however whereas that motif has a strong ascending bass line, this has a strong descending one, and part of its features are triplets and a dotted rhythm:

Ex. 1

Throughout the opera this motif is employed when knightly duty is discussed, and both De Bracy and Prince John are partly characterised by it. It first appears in full during the entrance of the knights in Act I scene 1, where its rather elastic dotted-note melody is extended to cover the long procession of knights and attendants. This is in the key of F-major, and it reappears in the same key for the entrance of Rowena. The use of the motif at such a point is rather mystifying: perhaps Sullivan was trying to convey the effect on the knights of Rowena's entrance – of their 'bold looks' directed at her. The music is also more heavily scored here, and has a full chorus, 'More light is there for lord and thrall/When lady fair comes into hall', so perhaps the chivalry of the knights is also implied.

The motif, now moving from G-minor to Bb, appears at the end of the Tournament scene when Prince John urges 'Sir Conqueror' to do his knightly duty. However the theme here is slightly different from other repeats, and more is made of the leaping interval at the end of the phrase:

Ex. 2

When De Bracy, in the second scene of Act II, proclaims that Rowena will be his 'honoured bride' the pattern of the notes is the same as their appearances in Act I, and in the same key (F-major). Finally, in a rather downcast B-minor, it is heard briefly as De Bracy is led in to hear his sentence from King Richard (III/2).

Another motif is the one allotted to Isaac the Jew. It accompanies his entrance in Act I, and this agitated and nervous little theme seems appropriate for the timid and gesturing Jew:

Ex. 3

This theme appears several times during the course of the opera: in the second scene of Act I, when Ivanhoe calls 'Isaac, Isaac I say', and when he (Isaac) rushes in at the end of the Glade scene to enlist Ivanhoe's aid for Rebecca. Here the theme is supported by an agitated bass line. Its final appearance is in the remaining moments of the opera, when Rebecca is released and joins Isaac. However Sullivan does not use the theme in the Ashby scene where Isaac pushes forward in the crowd and is greeted by Prince John's 'Isaac my Jew/my purse of Gold'. Perhaps Sullivan felt that the real importance here was in Prince John's taunt rather than in the appearance of the Jew himself.

One of the most important themes of the opera is the one called 'Ivanhoe's motif' by some commentators. This is perhaps more appropriately called the 'Pledge motif' because it symbolises the pledge of conflict between the Templar and Ivanhoe and accompanies each stage of that conflict. It first appears during the confrontation in Act I scene 1 when the Templar asks for a pledge from the Palmer (Ivanhoe in disguise) that when Ivanhoe returns from Palestine he will answer a challenge. The theme is sung first by the Templar:

Ex. 4

32

Ivanhoe replies in Db-major, and the Templar responds in A-major, neatly emphasising the gulf between them. When Rowena rises to support Ivanhoe the theme sounds again (in Eb) to underline the words 'Then I will speak and pledge my word'. It is extensively used in the Ashby scene when Ivanhoe rides to answer the challenge. The two-bar theme is firstly repeated several times, with Sullivan pushing up the key each time to suggest the growing excitement: Bb - C - D - Eb. Finally the theme blazes out in the brass (G-major) after the chorus have acclaimed the 'disinherited knight', underpinned by a dominant pedal which keeps the tension developing. The following words of both Friar Tuck and Locksley are underpinned by the theme, but surprisingly it plays no part in the subsequent combat sequence.

In the final scene of the opera the theme heralds the arrival of Ivanhoe, who is just in time to save Rebecca and fight the Templar. Both this fight and a previous one at the end of the Siege scene (III/1) are accompanied by a chromatically and rhythmically changed version of the motif, varied to make it more exciting for the situation. These are the only instances in the opera where a theme is fully transformed:

Ex. 5

Unifying Features Within a Scene

Several key melodic phrases are used by Sullivan within a scene, and are seldom heard again.

The opera opens with a phrase that dominates the first scene (Ex 6) but appears only once again, in the Ashby scene when De Bracy tells Prince John that Cedric is Thane of Rotherwood:

Ex. 6

This 'Rotherwood' theme epitomises Cedric's house. It makes its full impact in the introduction, where it is combined with a melody later appearing in Cedric's drinking song. The overlapping of the theme is particularly effective. It also makes a vigorous appearance in the chorus of men – 'Was hael'. However its final notes are used by Sullivan at the end of the scene for the words 'so ends the song', thus enclosing scene 1 with the same key (C-major) and similar linked music:

Ex. 7

Like the 'Norman Knight' motif, it is built on a simple triad, though its effect is more vigorous. It is perhaps a pity that Sullivan did not use this theme to characterise the Saxons throughout the opera.

The Ashby scene in Act I opens with music that suggests the wind blowing the flags on the tents of the competitors. This is underpinned by a Bb dominant pedal which leads into the chorus 'Will there be no more fighting?' This music reappears at several points in this scene:

Ex. 8

The scene is further unified by repeating the 'Plantagenesta!' chorus, first heard midway, at the end (although with different words).

The opera has many trumpet calls which appear at dramatic moments; Sullivan uses those which play a significant role in the Tournament (I/3) for effect in the siege of Torquilstone (III/1), where they characterise the Norman defenders. All these are built on triadic figures:

Ex. 9

The Copmanhurst scene in Act II has a couple of themes which play an important part in the musical development. The first one is used and developed extensively, and suggests "the very air of the forest" (J. Fuller-Maitland, review in *The Times,* Monday 2 February 1891).

Ex. 10

The second is the ecclesiastical strain that introduces the character of Friar Tuck. Here, Sullivan avoids sounding 'Victorian churchy' and suggests instead the musical world of Vaughan Williams. The theme certainly evokes the medieval church to which Tuck belongs:

Ex. 11

Each theme appears in the texture of the music at appropriate moments, and the first one is used as the basis for the short fugal episode during the eating of the venison pasty. Both of the themes' keys (D-major and F-major) are chosen for the characters' main songs during the scene: D-major for King Richard's 'I ask nor wealth' and F-major for Tuck's 'Ho, jolly Jenkin'.

In the first Torquilstone scene (II/2) Sullivan repeats the music from the introduction (Ex. 26 – now in the major key and slightly developed) after the brief trio 'In mercy save him' to cover the exit of the prisoners and the entrance of the Templar.

Phrases from the introduction to Act III scene 1 which lead into Ivanhoe's aria 'Happy with wingèd feet' reappear several times during the exchanges between Rebecca and Ivanhoe, but play no part in the 'siege' section which follows.

In the finale the opening sequence is unified by a short phrase in the minor which permeates the Grand Master's denouncement of Rebecca. It is used six times in all, and also forms the melodic line of Rebecca's '. . . and am content to die.'

Ex. 12A

Ex. 12B

Motivic Songs

Rather than a single key phrase, Sullivan also uses the melody of a song to establish character, give unity to a scene, or to link dramatic ideas. This is most evident in King Richard's case. In his first exchanges with Friar Tuck (I/3) he is the vigorous Black Knight, but after he has sung 'I ask nor wealth' the audience glimpses the other side to his character – the nature-loving merry monarch. The song is much used in the Glade scene (III/2), where the changes of words are most important, and its use – repeated three times in its original keys of D-major and B-major – gives a unifying aspect to the first part of the scene. The melody of the song is also used during the siege (III/1) when Ivanhoe asks of the progress of the 'Sable Knight'. At this point it is important that the audience knows to whom Ivanhoe is referring, and the use of the melody achieves just that. At the end of the opera, where Sullivan needs to emphasise Richard's kingly nobility, the melody is not used.

Ulrica's 'Whet the keen axes' neatly characterises that unfortunate old woman – its first appearance, in Act II scene 3 in the Turret Chamber of Torquilstone, beginning the scene and later accompanying her exit. Its subterranean murmurings are heard again at the beginning of Act III, when she leads Rebecca in to nurse the wounded Ivanhoe. On this occasion her ominous words 'Look to thy bridal torches' are emphasised by the melody, eerily played on low clarinets and bassoons. When at the height of the siege the castle begins to burn, Rebecca sings 'Now do I know thee, Fiend, with thy wedding torches', accompanied by a fragment of the melody. However, at the climax of the scene, when the song appears again, Sullivan effects a transformation. The key has been moved up a semitone to E-minor, and the opening words, 'Far leaps the fire-flame', have a new melody. This moves imperceptibly into the original melody, which is shared between soloist and orchestra. However this also has been changed, the dotted rhythm having been ironed out by triplets, and more use made of the rising phrase:

Whet the bright steel, then,   Sons of the Dra - gon!   Kin-dle the tor - ches, Daugh-ters of Hen - gist!

Ex. 13

Use of Recurring Phrases

At various moments in the opera Sullivan makes direct quotes of fragments of music previously heard. These are used to establish the relationship between one dramatic point and another. At other times he uses short melodic cells or harmonic features, sometimes slightly changed, as a device in the unifying process.

a) Direct quotes

Towards the end of the first scene, Cedric asks his Norman guests to pledge a toast – Sullivan slips in a couple of bars of the drinking song heard previously in the scene.

The sequence of sustained chords which underlines Isaac's opening solo in Act 1, at the words 'Isaac of York am I', is again used by Sullivan in the Glade scene at the words 'My child is doomed to die':

Ex. 14A

36

Ex. 14B

In Act II, when Friar Tuck taunts King Richard with 'Hast thou forgot thy valour?', the orchestra quotes the short theme which accompanied the King (disguised as the Black Knight) in the Ashby scene, and which appeared several times during his exchanges with Tuck.

During the siege of Torquilstone (III/1) Rebecca, who is describing the assault to Ivanhoe, twice makes a plea to the 'God of Israel' to 'shield us in this hour'. Sullivan emphasises the similarity by setting them both to the same melodic phrase in the minor.

In the Glade scene (III/2) Cedric and Rowena enter to music quoted from Act I scene 1, at the point when the Templar asks Rowena to 'Forgive, fair maid, the votaries of the sun'. The key has been changed from Bb to B-major, and although the orchestration is expanded it still makes effective use of the bass clarinet theme. The use of this music at this point is obviously Sullivan making a sly reference to the weather!

The finale contains a number of references to melodies which appear in other parts of the opera, and through them Sullivan is able to strengthen the dramatic and musical scheme. When Rebecca sings 'I am innocent' the orchestra underlines her following words with an important theme from her duet with the Templar, which is used to suggest her trust in God's deliverance (see Ex. 34). At the end of this sequence Sullivan portrays Rebecca's submission by eight gentle notes on the violins, which interestingly seem to quote the plainsong setting of the *Dies Irae*:

Ex. 15

At the climactic point, where the Templar tries once again to persuade Rebecca to allow him to rescue her, Sullivan quotes two significant melodies and overlaps them. The first is the melody of 'Woo thou thy snowflake' – flute above muted strings – and the 'Guard me' phrase from Rebecca's prayer as she sings her ascending line 'O Jehovah, guard me!' As the attendants tie her to the stake, strings alone – muted – play a moving section which recalls the melody she sang in the Ashby scene (I/3) to the words 'She groweth best where humble flowers bloom by lonely waters' – surely an association of words in portraying Rebecca's humble acceptance of her fate.

Sullivan's restraint at this point is noteworthy. In this situation a Wagner or a Verdi would probably have set rushing strings and harsh brass chords, but Sullivan's delicately muted strings are particularly sensitive. The unresolved cadence heightens the tension before the lower strings – on an unrelated A natural – begin the triplet pattern which heralds the dramatic appearance of Ivanhoe as Rebecca's champion. The whole effect of this sequence is especially moving.

During the romantic resolution of the finale Sullivan quotes two melodies: the first, from Rebecca's 'Ah would that thou and I' (III/1), reminds us of her love for Ivanhoe, and the second, neatly dovetailed in, repeats the theme of the second Ivanhoe/Rowena duet 'How oft beneath the far-off Syrian skies'. Both of these are in their original key of D-major.

The final chorus of the opera uses both the original key, B-major, and a melodic cadence from the quartet 'Forgive thy son' in the previous scene. This musical connection suggests that Sullivan felt that the values of the quartet – love and forgiveness – were exactly right to end the opera; and what better way than to quote music which reminds the listener of that important episode?

b) <u>Melodic and harmonic cells</u>

In Act I the first words of the Templar, which mention the 'soft almond eyes of Syrian girls', are underlined and followed by a phrase on the strings that includes an interval leap:

Ex. 16

This phrase is suggested later by Prince John in his exchanges with Rebecca – 'the Rose of Sharon'. The rising interval is evident throughout the scene, and becomes a feature of the whole episode:

Ex. 17

One of the Wagnerian influences in the first scene takes the form of a feminine cadence (in which the melodic resolution of the final chord is slightly delayed). This harmony and pattern of notes (Ex. 18) is used twice after the 'Norman Knight' music – once for the knights, and once for Rowena. It then appears again, in C-major, after the long flowing melody on the strings following the exit of Cedric and Rowena (Ex. 18A):

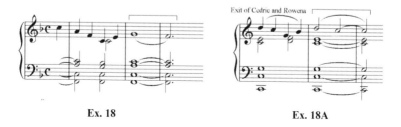

Ex. 18   Ex. 18A

A slightly changed melodic variation is used just as the chorus 'And so to sleep' begins, and occurs twice during this:

Ex. 18B

The cadence also occurs at the end of De Bracy's 'Was it not so, Sir Templar?' and at his squire's words earlier in the scene, 'Cedric of Rotherwood' (Ex. 18D):

Ex. 18C   Ex. 18D

Its influence is felt again in Act III, when Richard pardons De Bracy and admonishes him to 'live in honesty':

Ex. 18E

However the melodic (not harmonic) content of 'Cedric of Rotherwood' (Ex. 18D) is echoed in Rowena's 'A kind goodnight to all' (Ex. 18F), and the final cadence of the scene (I/1) also seems influenced by this. Rowena's exact phrase also momentarily appears in the second scene of Act I, after Ivanhoe has said his farewells (Ex. 18G):

Ex. 18F   **Ex. 18G**

One interesting piece of melodic similarity concerns three phrases sung by Ivanhoe at different moments in the opera, but all regarding 'love' or 'caring'. The chromatic quality of each phrase is evident, and they seem to suggest the gentle side of his nature. The first appears during the exchanges with Rowena in Act I scene 2, when he regrets that he knows little of the knight – 'since thou dost care to hear of him'. This melodic phrase, together with its key and harmony, is almost exactly mirrored in the Glade scene (III/2) when Ivanhoe sings to Richard 'Thy love is more to me, my King'. Another suggestion of the phrase appears during the siege (III/1) when Ivanhoe begs Rebecca not to risk her life for him, or 'My whole life long should I go mourning thee':

Ex. 19A

Ex. 19B   **Ex. 19C**

The 'Syrian' Influence

Several characters in the opera share a common link with the Middle East, either because of their place of origin, like Isaac and Rebecca, or having fought in the Crusades like King Richard, Ivanhoe, and the Templar with his following of 'dusky knaves'. Sullivan responds to this by suggesting melodically, with a chromatic turn of phrase, the characters' connection with that region. To the listener there is also a sense that Sullivan is taking the melody in an unexpected direction. Rebecca's 'Guard me' phrase is the most obvious, but the influence can also be seen in the 'Pledge' motif and at the climax of the 'Syrian skies' duet for Ivanhoe and Rowena.

All three melodic phrases have the same harmonic chord base of tonic major/subdominant minor/tonic major. This can be seen when all three are transposed into the key of Eb:

Ex. 20A   Ex. 20B

Ex. 20C

The same harmonic basis can be heard in the Tournament scene, when the crowd hails the nameless knight – Ivanhoe in disguise – as victor in the lists:

Ex. 21

There is a suggestion of this harmonic sequence in the Grand Master's phrase in the finale (Ex. 12A), and in the Templar's 'Woo thou thy snowflake' at the words 'Draws the full tide of my rebellious blood', the B double flat (A natural) instead of the expected Bb gives the melody a suggestive twist, and adds distinction to the phrase:

Ex. 22

41

Another unexpected note, but with a very different intended effect, is the one given to Friar Tuck just before he launches into 'Ho, jolly Jenkin'. The B natural on the word 'crow' in a Bb phrase is richly comic, and is a perfect note for the rotund friar to sing!

Ex. 23

Rhythmical Features

The use of triplets in the musical texture can be found in Sullivan's other works of the period, like the *Macbeth* music and *The Yeomen of the Guard*; but in *Ivanhoe* they permeate the whole opera. In the case of the Templar's music they are used as a tool towards characterisation, and help to emphasise his rather 'foreign' manner. His very first utterance in Act I suggests triplets by the flowing 6/4, but in his first words to Rowena they are evident in the vocal line. They are especially prominent in 'Woo thou thy snowflake', particularly at the words 'I will woo her', and they appear throughout the duet with Rebecca, effectively underlining the words 'Ere I would cease to claim thee mine own'.

Ex. 24

Triplets are also a feature of the 'Norman Knight' music, where they are combined with dotted notes. They are used particularly effectively in Cedric's drinking song (I/1) when the 'Knights of the Holy Order of the Temple' are toasted by De Bracy, and in the choral shout in praise of Rowena, 'All hail to our Lady Rowena':

Ex. 25

At the end of the first scene of Act I, in the beautifully scored 'Goodnight' music, the oscillating horn figure is in triplets. They are an important feature of the trumpet calls at Ashby, and appear in the vocal line of 'Plantagenesta!' and the chorus of Templars. Triplets are also effective in the melodic transformation of Ulrica's 'Whet the keen axes' at the end of the Siege scene (III/1). Here the change from a dotted rhythm clearly suggests the momentary ecstatic delirium of the character.

The use of dotted notes is most significant in martial or exciting moments. Their employment in the war song of Ulrica and the 'Norman Knight' music has been mentioned, and it is this rhythm which underpins much of the Siege scene. The agitation created by dotted notes is ideal for the trio which ends the Glade scene (III/2), and for the two sections of combat music for Ivanhoe and the Templar (see Ex. 5). The sense of agitation is also carried throughout the second scene of Act II, in Torquilstone Castle. Even the rhythm of the opening chords seems to utter the 'name of dread' – Torquilstone:

Allegro con brio

Ex. 26

Dotted notes appear not only in this introduction but also in Cedric's 'By heav'n, rather would I see this lady lifeless on her bier' (II/2) and after the brief trio before the Templar enters.

Unity of Individual Movements

Several of the self-contained numbers within an act are constructed with their own internal unity. This is especially so of the two large-scale duets: between Ivanhoe and Rowena (I/2) and the Templar and Rebecca (II/3).

The duet between Ivanhoe and Rowena, 'If thou dost see him', is one of Sullivan's most perfect and expressive lyrical outpourings, especially when one remembers that it is a love duet in which only one of the characters knows the identity of the other (Ivanhoe is in disguise as a Palmer). Nevertheless Sullivan shows the bond between them by the music. He prepares for the duet's musical content earlier in the scene, when Ivanhoe responds to Rowena's 'Rise, Holy Palmer,' and the strings and flutes have a falling phrase (Ex. 27A) that is destined to become an integral part of the musical fabric of the duet (Ex. 27B):

Ex. 27A

Ex. 27B

When the duet begins it is clear that Sullivan is responding to the words 'restless sea' – 'ocean foam' – 'barren sea' as his inspiration. The rising and falling of the phrases, the luscious orchestration, the chromatic harmony all combine to create the picture of a changing seascape. The voices seem buoyed up like boats on a wave; the falling phrase quoted above (Ex. 27B) begins to permeate the orchestral textures in Ivanhoe's section ('Ah then if he beyond the ocean foam'), and when the voices join together this falling phrase is given to them while the cellos, bassoons, violas and clarinets carry the opening melody – an inspired moment, and one which concludes the section in a satisfying musical way:

Ex. 28

The coda as the lovers make their farewells is given a sense of mystery and longing by phrases on the clarinets and bassoons over a tonic pedal of F. It is interesting to note that one of the short ascending phrases of the duet, first heard after Rowena's 'Tell him there are those that think of him', appears several times in the second duet for the lovers in Act III scene 2. It is played on exactly the same instruments – clarinets and bassoons (Ex. 29 A/B). This second duet, which is less complex, also shows the pattern of one voice per verse, with both joining together towards the end.

Ex. 29A

Ex. 29B

'Lord of Our Chosen Race' and the duet for Rebecca and the Templar

Rebecca's prayer, 'Lord of our Chosen Race,' really needs to be viewed as an introduction to the duet, for not only does it provide the main key scheme – the Ab-minor/major axis – but also frames the duet, being both the beginning and the ending of the sequence.

The Prayer has two verses in Ab-minor, and Sullivan varies the second one by introducing a counter-theme for the cor anglais – an interesting choice of instrument because it also plays an important role in the dark colouring of the Templar's 'Woo thou thy snowflake'.

Much has been made of the fact that Sullivan gave this song a special eastern 'feel' by borrowing the musical phrase 'Guard me' from one he heard chanted by a minister in the Old Jewish Synagogue in Leipzig during his student days:

Ex. 30

However the whole aria has a distinctly Jewish 'tone' throughout, and Sullivan achieves this by using wide intervals in the melody line, especially at the beginning, where a feeling of longing and melancholy is achieved.

Comparing the opening phrase with a modern evocation of Jewishness – the theme from *Schindler's List* by John Williams, shows that Williams achieved his effects in a similar way. The short harmonic rising phrase towards the cadence is an interesting coincidence, as is the fact that Williams uses a solo viola for his theme, the very same instrument that Sullivan uses for the complex repeated rhythm in the first two verses (see Ex. 36):

Ex. 31A

Ex. 31B

The use of the wide interval also appears earlier in this scene, when Rebecca asks of Ulrica 'Is there no way of safety?'

Ex. 32

The same melodic phrase appears in the bass line when Ulrica responds, 'No way but through the gates of death.'

For the final verse of the prayer the key plunges gloriously into Ab-major, and Sullivan brings back the 'Guard me' phrase in the orchestra while Rebecca climbs to a high pianissimo Bb. A truly wonderful moment.

The little triplet figure at the words 'deeps of the sea' and 'heights of the air' (Ex. 33A) is used by Sullivan as the basis of the dramatic music when Rebecca is carried off by the Templar at the end of the Siege (Ex. 33B). It reappears at the end of the opera when Ivanhoe fights the Templar as Rebecca's champion:

O Thou, who know'st the deeps o' the sea And climb - est the heights o' the air,

Ex. 33A

Ex. 33B

This final section is also the inspiration for a passage of Rebecca's music later in the Siege scene of Act 3 where, at the words 'Not thus did Judah's warriors go', the key Ab-major, rhythm of the melody and the harp arpeggio accompaniment all match the aria.

As the prayer finishes, the Templar enters, accompanied by the melody of his aria 'Woo thou thy snowflake' in the orchestra, and the duet begins. Without doubt this duet between Rebecca and the Templar is the dramatic core of the opera, and Sullivan rose to the challenge to provide some of his finest dramatic music. In simple terms this duet corresponds to the pattern of the others – the voices sing separately until the end, when they join together and sweep the scene and the Act to a triumphant close.

The duet consists of six sections, each exploring a different aspect of the relationship and conflict. Sullivan binds the whole together by the use of an important melodic phrase which suggests Rebecca's defiance of the Templar, and her faith in God's redemption:

Ex. 34

The base key of the whole duet is the Ab-minor/major axis, and generally Rebecca pulls the key back to this axis in her responses to the Templar. The theme (Ex. 34) is first introduced after the Templar's avowal of love, and it permeates the section in which he appeals to the cross and Rebecca proclaims her Jewish faith. However the Templar tires of this – 'Preach me no more' – and the agitated music, together with a change of key from flats to sharps, signals the change of mood. At his words 'Yield to thy fate' Sullivan supports the Templar with a fortissimo 'stopped' chord on the horns. A very ominous sound which adds to Rebecca's terror! However, undaunted, she proclaims that '. . . . the God of Abraham opens a path of safety', whereupon the main theme sounds in the woodwind and leads to the dramatic climax during which she threatens to throw herself from the battlements.

The Templar's unexpected response is a declaration of his ambition to make Rebecca 'Empress of the East'. His words, 'My mailèd foot shall climb the throne of kings', are underlined by an insidious curling phrase on the lower strings and bassoons, which leads to his final rhapsodical outburst. Rebecca again leads the key back to Ab-minor as she rejects his suggestions, and the theme now appears against an agitated rhythmic background:

Ex. 35

This passes through various keys and leads to another climax which is interrupted by the call to arms.

The final section, marked *con fuoco e sempre animato* shows a variation and extension of the theme over a slow-moving triplet bass line, which leads finally to the joining together of voices, creating a massive dramatic climax. As the Templar leaves, Rebecca sings a moving rise to a Bb (now forte) and the orchestra thunders out the 'Guard me' phrase from her aria.

There is no doubt that Sullivan's success in this duet depends very much on his use of the melodic phrase (Ex. 34) as a unifying feature. The particular quality of this phrase, especially its chromatic construction, allows it to be easily developed in order to facilitate freedom of harmonic modulation; Sullivan brilliantly expands this phrase to mirror every changing mood of this wonderful duet.

47

Characterisation of Individuals

By using the techniques discussed above Sullivan was able to achieve some notable characterisations of individual people, despite the fact that in the libretto, and the novel for that matter, many of the characters are only at best rather sketchy. Isaac of York, whose role in the novel is considerably trimmed by Sturgis, does have his own motif to help his identity, and Ulrica is strongly characterised by the use of her Saxon war-song. Certain characters, like Prince John and the Grand Master only appear briefly, but Sullivan was still able to impart some identity to their music. Only poor Locksley seems to lack some sort of identity.

Through the course of the opera Sullivan shows the change in Cedric from the vigorous defender of Saxon pride in Act I to the defeated man of Acts II and III, when he finally forgives his son.

De Bracy is more successfully characterised by the music Sullivan gives to him, and this is helped by the use of the 'Norman Knight' motif (Ex. 1). He is rather a cynic, and the lightweight music given to him tells us so. Only in the scene of his trial before Richard (III/2) does the music suggest a discomfited man – though the words show he has not lost his sense of humour. It is interesting to compare the setting of the opening words of De Bracy and the Templar in Act I scene 1 to see how skilfully Sullivan delineates the two different natures.

King Richard is mainly characterised through his song, which reveals him as the troubadour king of romance; his martial nature is described, but not given direct musical expression. Friar Tuck's ecclesiastical status is suggested in his opening phrase, while his jovial nature needs no further expression than the most popular song in the opera – 'Ho, jolly Jenkin'. With both King Richard and Friar Tuck, Sullivan allows room for development by intelligent character actors.

The characterisation of the lovers Ivanhoe and Rowena is less defined than might be expected, though this is a clear reflection of the novel. Sullivan does, however, attempt to give each of them an heroic as well as a lyrical aspect, and he does give them some of the must beautiful music in the opera: Rowena's soliloquy to the moon, and the duet which follows. This scene is paralleled in Act III when Ivanhoe sings to the dawning day – 'Happy with wingèd feet'. Ivanhoe's other song, 'Like mountain lark', shows the vigorous, manly side of his nature, and there are many heroic moments in the opera to show his strength. Rowena too is given strong phrases, especially when she rises in the Hall of Rotherwood to defend the apparently absent Ivanhoe. On the whole it is the humanity of Rowena which most touches, of which the aria and duet in Act I are the supreme examples.

But the dominant characters in the opera, as in the novel, are the Templar and Rebecca, and with them Sullivan rises magnificently to create characters of flesh and blood. From the beginning he seems to be preparing for the great duet. The first words of the Templar are in Ab-major (I/1) and the first words of Rebecca are in Ab-minor (I/3), thus immediately making the connection with the Ab-major/minor axis of the duet. Both the wonderful monologue for the Templar and Rebecca's prayer add to the compelling picture. Rebecca's hatred of the Templar, expressed in the dark Ab-major/minor keys, is contrasted by Sullivan with her love for Ivanhoe (in 'Ah would that thou and I might lead our sheep' Act III scene 1 - words taken from the Song of Solomon) which is expressed in the remote key of D-major.

This aria is a *tour de force* for the singer, with a strongly contrasted middle-section beginning at 'My Asahel, O swift as the wild roe' and ending with the section 'A bird, his glad song winging up to high heaven', when Sullivan's orchestra takes on a 20th century impressionistic glow. It is an amazing moment which stands out starkly from the rest of the aria.

Characterisation of the Chorus

When one considers Sullivan's wonderful portrayal of various groups in the Savoy operas, the writing for the chorus in *Ivanhoe* seems disappointing. They are used as a 'Jack of all Trades' to support the action rather than showing strong character in their own right. The ladies, especially, have little to do, appearing in only two scenes (unless one counts the behind-scenes call 'Room for the Lady Rowena' in Act I scene 1). In the Tournament scene the chorus 'Plantagenesta!', a celebration of the dynasty of King Richard, makes its impact by being the first extended piece of full choral writing in the opera, and an example of Sullivan's favourite device – the double chorus – combining two different themes.

As far as the chorus is concerned *Ivanhoe* is definitely a man's opera, and Sullivan is successful in exploiting the particular quality of men's voices, especially in the first scene of Act I, in which Cedric's retainers are defined by the chorus 'Was hael' and the drinking song. Later they play a significant role in the exchanges between Ivanhoe and the Templar. At the end of the scene they are used to create atmosphere (the 'Goodnight' sequence) and this usage occurs again in the Glade scene (III/2) where the woodland 'feel' is achieved by the chorus 'Light foot upon the dancing green'.

The Templars' chorus which opens the opera's final scene is a splendidly sonorous piece of writing. Sullivan depicts not the mysterious, dark side of their nature, but the glory and pomp in a G-major setting which reflects the words *'Nobis sit victoria, Nostro Templo gloria, Gloria sancto nomini! – Let ours be the victory, Glory to our Temple, Glory to the Sacred name!'*

Much of the choral writing is strongly reminiscent of the block harmony of *The Yeomen of the Guard*, especially in the use of the four part men's chorus; but throughout the opera there are touches which create interest – the outburst in praise of the Temple Knights in Cedric's drinking song, the choral greeting to Rowena at Ashby, the short section of imitation that emerges from the texture in the middle of 'Light foot upon the dancing green', and the eerie unison chromatic passage – 'A judgement!' – following the death of the Templar.

Harmony

Many interesting aspects of the harmonic style and its contribution to the twin aims of unity and contrast have been examined during the course of this article, and certainly much of the general characterisation stems from Sullivan's flexibility in determining the appropriate musical setting for a situation. Chromaticism allows him to move freely within a framework, and this is particularly useful in conveying the shifting emotions during the more intimate moments of a scene. The score has many instances of enharmonic modulations, some of which are used expressively, as when Ivanhoe appears before Rowena in Act I scene 2, or at Rebecca's words 'And I no more behold the light of day,' (Act I scene 3) when the change occurs on the word 'light' and gives an expressive glow to the melody. The entrance of the Templar after Rebecca's prayer is another good example of effective change. Other modulations which occur on pivotal notes are used for dramatic effect, such as happens twice in the Tournament Scene, in which the pivotal note 'D' changes the key from Bb to G at the lead-in to the chorus 'Plantagenesta!' and just before the choral greeting to Rowena.

The use of more diatonic harmony gives the open air scenes a sense of space, and one suspects that Sullivan fully realised that good character actors would need flexibility in such a scene as the one between Friar Tuck and King Richard (II/1). The score at this point eschews thick chromatic textures, though an occasional touch like the modulation from A-major to

Db-major via Ab-major at Richard's words 'The wine cup thou didst not refuse' adds a welcome sparkle.

The use of dominant and tonic pedals also plays its part in creating atmosphere and mood. Dominant pedals are used specifically to create a sense of anticipation, as in the opening of the Tournament scene, where Sullivan maintains a dominant pedal for twenty bars until the words 'Who comes here?' introduce a change of harmony, the lead-in to the chorus 'Plantagenesta!', and in several other scenes. At other times they create a sense of action being continued, as in the climax to the ensemble in the Siege scene between Rebecca, Ivanhoe and the chorus, where the pedal is maintained for twenty-one bars. In Rebecca's prayer a dominant pedal is maintained in the inner parts in the shape of a rhythmically complex ostinato for the violas:

Ex. 36

Tonic pedals are used more extensively, and tend to create a feeling of contentment. This is true of the introduction to the Glade scene, the coda of the first Rowena/Ivanhoe duet, and when Cedric embraces Ivanhoe after forgiving him (III/2). It creates a very dreamy mood in the final part of the 'Goodnight' music (I/1), and yet sounds joyful when used as a basis for the choral greeting to Rowena – 'Our Saxon princess! Hail!' – in Act I scene 3. When used during particular songs it is most successful in 'Woo thou thy snowflake', where the interest is created by the movement of the inner harmonies – as it is in Ulrica's 'Whet the keen axes'. It is less successful in Rebecca's 'Ah would that thou and I might lead our sheep', because the unchanging harmony does not allow the melody to develop sufficiently to avoid becoming rather static.

For dramatic moments Sullivan generally relies on two main harmonic devices – the diminished seventh chord and the stepwise ascending sequence of chords. The combination of the two can be seen in Ulrica's 'In this cursed place' (II/3), and the second device can be seen three times during the Ashby Scene: the entrance of Ivanhoe, the chorus 'Alas, poor boy,' and the lead-in to Prince John's 'Off with his helmet, heralds'. It can also be clearly seen at the moment when Rebecca sees the flames engulfing the castle – 'What angry redness' – and during the build-up to her threat to throw herself from the window during the confrontation duet (II/3). The diminished seventh is employed for numerous climactic moments, a typical example being the 'Ah!' from the chorus as Ulrica throws herself from the battlements during the Siege scene (III/1). The chord also informs much of the harmonic structure during the combat in the lists, and for the seizure of Rebecca by the Templar at the height of the siege of Torquilstone.

Summary

A detailed and careful study of the score of *Ivanhoe* reveals that Sullivan, with his twin compositional aims of contrast and unity, forms the work into a far more consistent and homogeneous structure than has previously been acknowledged by commentators. Certainly the methods he employed here are well in advance of anything he had previously used in opera, except perhaps in *The Yeomen of the Guard*. In fact the music of *Ivanhoe* is an obvious extension and development of that written for *Yeomen*, the influence of which can be seen in the Act I choruses, and especially in 'If ladies' love' from the Ashby scene. However in *Ivanhoe* the whole scope of the vocal writing, word-setting and melody is freer and much more expansive. The general 'tone' of the work is lyrical rather than dramatic, and perhaps critics of the time were responding to this when they declared that 'from first to last the work is, in a musical sense, astonishingly beautiful.' (*Black & White* 6 February 1891.) Sullivan must have recognised this emphasis on the lyrical when he titled his work a 'Romantic Opera'; perhaps if he had called it a 'Lyric Opera', and steered D'Oyly Carte away from using 'Grand' in the title, future misunderstanding of the work's content would have been avoided.

By viewing *Ivanhoe* as a lyrical opera we can see it as an historical precursor of the operas of Delius (*Irmelin* [1892] and *Koanga* [1895]), Stanford's later operas (*Much Ado About Nothing* [1901] had Sturgis as its librettist), Boughton's *The Immortal Hour* and Vaughan Williams (especially *The Pilgrim's Progress* which has a dramatic framework similar to *Ivanhoe*) – all works in which the lyrical is more dominant than the dramatic. After the 1973 Beaufort Opera revival of *Ivanhoe* the reviewer Michael Greenhalgh noted that the accompaniment of Rowena's 'O moon art thou clad' and the following duet with Ivanhoe are "of a glowing warm variety not found again in quite the same fashion until Delius (I am thinking particularly of the closing scene of *Koanga*)." Certainly the beauty of the orchestration in *Ivanhoe* has always been acknowledged, proving that Sullivan was well divorced from the heavy Brahmsian scoring of some of his contemporaries. Further affinity with Delius is found in Sullivan's ability to suggest a mood. The critics who mentioned the 'fresh air of England' present in some scenes of *Ivanhoe* recognised this ability, and here Sullivan is in sympathy with the imagery of Scott:

> The daylight had dawned upon the glades of the oak forest. The green boughs glittered with all their pearls of dew. The hind led her fawn from the covert of high fern to the more open walks of the greenwood . . . (Opening of Chapter 32)

One has only to compare 'Light foot upon the dancing green' with the opening chorus of Act II of Marschner's *Der Templer und die Jüdin,* also set in the forest, to sense the particularly English atmosphere of the former. In the 20th century Britten's *Gloriana* has an affinity with *Ivanhoe* – but more of that elsewhere.

Sullivan's musical palette is generally as well suited to the setting of atmosphere and mood as it is responsive to the lyrical, intimate episodes. Sturgis was fully aware of this, and he provided many such opportunities for the composer. However the wonderful duet for the Templar and Rebecca shows that, given the right stimulus, Sullivan was also able to write dramatically developed music; other dramatic moments, like the Act I confrontation between Ivanhoe and the Templar, are also well managed. The scene in the lists and the siege of Torquilstone are perhaps less successful, and are exciting – no doubt about that! – in a more superficial way. In these episodes, of course, the arts of the stage manager and set designer are predominant, as Sullivan well knew.

The several light-hearted scenes which the opera provides, like the exchanges between King Richard and Friar Tuck, are also successfully set by Sullivan without resorting to self-caricature. It has been suggested that Wamba the Jester was eliminated because Sullivan did not want an association with another character like Jack Point (*Yeomen of the Guard*). However we know that Wamba *was* included as a non-singing part (he is mentioned by Percy Anderson, the designer, and is individually credited in the German production) – and it is more likely that his part was compressed for reasons of time. Certainly the time element influences the work in other ways. Sullivan must have been aware during composition that quite lengthy periods of time would be required for the scene changes (twenty minutes after the Siege scene) and no doubt he felt it would be unwise to provide an overture and orchestral interludes to link scenes. This may also be the reason why several sections do not receive the sort of extended operatic treatment one would expect, though it is more likely that Sullivan was responding to the balance of the opera as a whole.

This balance is carefully calculated by Sturgis to do full justice to the novel in its entirety, and by such a method there are gains and losses. On the one hand it meant that Sullivan was unable to concentrate fully on certain characters, as Marschner does in *Der Templer und die Jüdin* (although it has to be said that the original version of that long opera is a dramatic shambles); on the other hand the balance of the story is consistently maintained and followed through. For instance the finale has generally been derided, and the death of the Templar is indeed a particularly difficult moment. However by not giving particular prominence to any one character (Rebecca for example) Sullivan and Sturgis maintain their aim of staging the novel as Scott left it. Sullivan mentions a more 'sombre ending' to the opera, which may have been a fuller realisation of Rebecca's fate, but this was 'taken out,' probably to stay more within the terms of the original conception, even at the cost of operatic effectiveness. The same stress on the story is seen elsewhere in the opera: for instance, the love of Rebecca for Ivanhoe is expressed in solo form – 'Ah would that thou and I' – rather than the more operatically effective duet. This is as it is in Scott – Rebecca never expresses her love openly. Also, in the Tournament Scene when Ivanhoe is unmasked, one might have expected the operatic convention of a long ensemble, with each character expressing different feelings. Instead the scene moves quickly to its close, while the merry strains of the chorus cover the dismay of the main characters (which Maitland noted was similar to the ending of *Carmen*.)

Winton Dean, in his review in *The Musical Times* of the 1973 revival of *Ivanhoe*, wrote that the Copmanhurst scene is 'dramatically irrelevant.' This is perfectly true, but it does show a complete misunderstanding of the aims of Sullivan and Sturgis. Their intention to stick close to the novel meant that this scene *had* to be included, for it is such a familiar part of the novel, as well as allowing a period of respite from the action – Marschner also includes this scene, in which he set Scott's poem *The Song of the Barefooted Friar*. Generally, Sturgis relies on his audience's familiarity with the novel, and for this reason concentrates on making attractive stage pictures rather than telling the story, and this tends to give a static, tableau effect. It is this tableau effect which modern commentators have most difficulty in accepting; they therefore criticise Sullivan for making little or no attempt to unify the opera beyond the scope of a primitive *leitmotiv* – certainly a false and damaging premise. Even Thomas F. Dunhill, usually Sullivan's champion, called *Ivanhoe* 'a mere panorama of events without constructive unity.' This particular chestnut has been trotted out by many critics who have not bothered to study the opera at all, or question the validity of this statement.

Sullivan's compositional aims in *Ivanhoe* are strongly bound to his hope for a popular success, and a characteristic English Opera. He wanted people to be entertained, to be uplifted by the moral message, to be awed by the stage settings, and to go away whistling the tunes. He wanted his music to reach the heart not the head, and to be free from the foreign styles which dogged most of the English operas of the period. He chose the best elements of the German, French, and Italian operatic traditions when it suited him, mixed them well with the English Ballad-Opera tradition, and produced an opera which is consistent within itself. Most importantly, he avoided writing in a style of opera which he had spent a lifetime parodying.

Ivanhoe stands apart in Sullivan's works, and contains some of his finest music. It is a work which, though designed to be popular, does not yield its treasures in one or two hearings.

Familiarity with the score brings many delights, which probably accounts for its initial success, and caused people to return again and again during the original run. The Victorians knew and loved their Scott, and in *Ivanhoe* they had their favourite novel presented on stage in the most beautiful scenic pictures, accompanied by melodious and fluent music. The sort of pleasure this afforded them must have been very similar to the pleasure experienced today when one sees a novel like *The Lord of the Rings* made into wonderful films.

This was Sullivan's ultimate aim, and in order to recreate in terms of 'national' music the historical ideals embodied in Scott's novel, he singlemindedly pursued his course, even to the extent of ignoring operatic convention and trends. He was rewarded at the time with a legitimate and undeniable success. *Ivanhoe* is not, and is not intended as, a strenuously heroic opera, but it is truly a *national* opera.

In his book on Victorian painters *And When Did You Last See Your Father?* Roy Strong makes the following observation:

> There is something deeply moving and courageous about the confidence with which they (the painters) evoke the visible past. It starts from a premise of self-possession and of security within the present totally unknown to us, which enables the painter's brush for a brief period to defy time as it moved triumphantly through it.

For 'painter's brush' read 'composer's art', and we have what might be a perfect description of Sullivan's aims and achievements in *Ivanhoe*.

ACT 3 SCENE 1 – REBECCA AND IVANHOE

'Ah! Would that thou and I might lead our sheep'

THE

ROYAL ENGLISH OPERA.

Sole Proprietor and Manager,
R. D'OYLY CARTE.

IVANHOE

(Adapted from Sir Walter Scott's Novel)

A Romantic Opera,

IN THREE ACTS

Words by

JULIAN STURGIS.

Music by

ARTHUR SULLIVAN.

ACT 1 SCENE 1 – CEDRIC'S HALL AT ROTHERWOOD

ACT 1 SCENE 3 – THE LISTS AT ASHBY

ACT 2 SCENE 1 - THE FRIAR'S CELL AT COPMANHURST

'Ho Jolly Jenkin'

ACT 2 SCENE 2 – A PASSAGE-WAY IN TORQUILSTONE

INSET: ACT 3 SCENE 2 – IN THE FOREST

ACT II
SCENE III.

REBECCA.

O FOR THE WINGS
OF WHICH THE PSALMIST SINGS THAT
I MIGHT FLY
AND HIDE ME FROM ALL EYES.

ACT 2 SCENE 3 – A TURRET-CHAMBER IN TORQUILSTONE

ACT 2 SCENE 3

'Stand Back, Proud Man'

ACT 3 SCENE 1 – THE STORMING OF TORQUILSTONE

ACT 3 SCENE 3 TEMPLESTOWE- DEATH OF THE TEMPLAR

FINALE – STAGE PHOTOPGRAPH

Courtesy of Mr Melvin Tarran

IVANHOE

Written by
HARRY WRIGHT,

Composed by
G. DURANDEAU,

Sung with Great Success by

WALTER MUNROE.

Copyright

LONDON:
B. MOCATTA & Co.
37 Berners St W.
Stannard & Son lith

Price 4/-

1 Now ladies do not think for a moment I'm a single man
I am married I must own it really married that I am
My wife is not exactly master but to hear her jaw
To see the way that I give in you think her word was law.
She reads my evening paper in the daytime when I'm out
And one of them has caused this trouble there can be no doubt
She said to Cartes she'd made up her mind she meant to go
And that's the reason why I took her to see Ivanhoe.

Ivanhoe Ivanhoe my wife said she meant to go
She said it must be Irish for she read it was Oily Cartes show
So off we went and a good night spent
But it cost me over four weeks rent
And out of my house I've got to go
But never mind I seen Ivanhoe.

2.

She made up her mind one evening that to the theatre she'd go
So off we started arm in arm to see this Ivanhoe
She said the gallery that would do she would not be denied
And so to reach the gallery door my very best I tried.
As that was full we tried the pit but that was just the same
She blackguarded the people though none of them were to blame
The stalls dress circle all alike she would not go away
To keep her quiet four pounds four for a box I had to pay. *Chorus &c*

3.

They made her take her bonnet off which at first she refused to do
I thought she'd loose her temper and kick up a hullibaloo
I talked to her and wheedled round her like a sly old fox
She gave her bonnet up and then we walked into the box.
She saw a programme then she turned round to me with a smile
You told me this was English but its Irish all the while
Oiley Carte he's the master Mr Sullivan wrote the play
O'Mara sings and I think they're all Irish anyway. *Chorus &c*

4.

The band struck up and what a band its elegant that's a fact
The curtain rose and what a treat to hear them sing and act
My wife kept shouting out bravo which attention seemed to call
For eyes were turned towards our box from almost ev'ry stall.
However we got home all right with every farthing spent
Next day the landlord called and said that he must have his rent
No rent to give so from my house I am compelled to go
I don't care one brass farthing for I have seen Ivanhoe. *Chorus &c*

THE · PENNY
No. 1549—Vol. 60   FEBRUARY 7, 1891

ILLUSTRATED · PAPER
AND + ILLUSTRATED TIMES

REGISTERED AT THE GENERAL POST OFFICE AS A NEWSPAPER.

London: Printed and Published at the Office, 10, Milford-lane, Strand, in the Parish of St. Clement Danes, in the County of London, by Thomas Fox, 10, Milford-lane, Strand, aforesaid.

DEATH OF BRIAN.

IVANHOE AND CONTINENTAL OPERA

by Jonathan Strong

Nabucco (Milan, 9 March 1842)
Arthur Sullivan (born London, 13 May 1842)
Der fliegende Holländer (Dresden, 2 January 1843)

Our composer was born just as the two great masters were beginning to revolutionize the art of music drama, Verdi by a gradual expansion of its conventions, Wagner with daring leaps into new forms and harmonies. At the height of their powers, these two men so dominated their native schools that today little else stands out from the Italian or German repertories of those years. Verdi and Wagner were then and remain today the pillars of nineteenth-century grand opera. When Sullivan finally came to add his own contribution, Wagner had been laid to rest in Bayreuth and Verdi, silent since *Aida*, had just brought forth *Otello,* and who could have imagined the old man still had *Falstaff* in him? It was a significant point in operatic history, a time for reassessment.

No single dominant figure had arisen in France to transform the art of Auber and Meyerbeer as Verdi had Rossini's and Wagner Weber's, though under more receptive circumstances it might have been Berlioz. Working more congenially within the French system, Gounod did effect a bridge between *opéra comique* and grand opera by replacing the dialogs in *Faust* with recitatives; later, Ernest Guiraud did the same for *Carmen* and *Les Contes d'Hoffmann*, further blurring the once exclusive categories. It was Sullivan's exact contemporary Massenet who arrived at a more original synthesis in his *Manon* by underscoring the spoken text with continuous music, a practice he unfortunately did not employ again.

While the Russian Glinka and the Czech Smetana created their national operas out of fairy tales, village romances, and historical pageants, the English were saddled with a problematic tradition. Perhaps, the Slavs benefited by starting afresh from an easier intimacy with their folk culture. England imagined itself more sophisticated, and yet since the death of Purcell, the homegrown musical theater had been reduced largely to ballad opera, which in the nineteenth century turned naturally into an anglicized version of *opéra comique* as practiced by men like Balfe, Wallace, and Benedict. Then, just as John Gay had once subverted the Italian opera, Arthur Sullivan began undermining accepted operatic conventions through ironic parody, after which it was impossible for him (or any other Britisher) to write a serious English-language opera of quite the old sort ever again.

An operatic tradition may be fostered but not calculated. *Der Freischütz*, *A Life for the Tsar*, and *The Bartered Bride* each founded a native school when it was greeted spontaneously as an embodiment of the national spirit by its early audiences. Sullivan himself achieved something of that effect with *Trial by Jury,* the most stageworthy British opera since that other breach-of-promise drama, *Dido and Aeneas,* and with each new work with Gilbert, Sullivan took a step further from a pastiche of continental models and brought to perfection an inimitable genre of comic opera at the Savoy. When he was at last presented with the prospect of yet a second opera house to be built expressly for his work, he was thoroughly prepared to discover how to write grand opera in English. He stated his intention to seek a compromise between the three major continental schools, but the results in *Ivanhoe* do not sound like a mere compromise. Rather, Sullivan's intimate sense of Victorian musical taste, nurtured by a quarter century in the theater, drew him to fashion out of familiar materials a new operatic form that would surprise, delight, and move audiences who had never heard those elements assembled in quite that way before.

It has been remarked, by way of dismissing *Ivanhoe*, that it appeared just as *Cavalleria Rusticana* was pointing the way to a new generation of opera composers. But the problems faced by Mascagni and Sullivan were not, at heart, so dissimilar. The younger man, having labored long over his *Guglielmo Ratcliff*, responded to the challenge of the Sanzogno competition with an entirely new sort of Italian opera, an intimate drama, elaborated in choral and instrumental mood pieces and ballads, that built, as in Greek tragedy, to one searing dramatic climax. Sullivan's work is structured like a novel, as Donizetti's Scottish opera decidedly is not. *Ivanhoe* presents itself in nine tableaux with a panoply of characters and no single dramatic event. Like Mascagni, Sullivan had to take a fresh look at his public's sensibility and, under considerable financial pressure, determine what would speak to it in a way that recent English works from the Carl Rosa Company had failed to do. So he took from his comic operas what came so naturally to him, the choruses and ballads, and kept them brief and shapely. Also brief by grand opera standards were the ensembles such as the Act II trio or the quartet in Act III; only the duet scene for the Templar and Rebecca came near to Verdian dimensions, depicting a favorite Victorian theme, virtue assaulted, but with the crisis averted.

The story moves right along, and the music never dawdles. Accustomed to Gilbert's extended finales, Sullivan desired to propel each scene forward and not allow the meditative elaborations he had parodied in earlier years nor reach for the eroticism of Wagner or the tragic passion of Verdi . He kept his recitative passages short, too, and moved quickly into arioso, as in the Templar's "Since I took ship from Palestine" or the little exchange between John and Rebecca. The Act III love duet remains modest in proportion, and in the final scene the moment where Ivanhoe turns from Rebecca to Rowena passes as quickly as the two women's motifs. These are but a few examples to show that, after a period when continental opera was expanding its sense of time, Sullivan held to an English appreciation of concision and understatement, a quality notable in the twentieth-century operas of Vaughan Williams and Britten. In *Ivanhoe* there is plenty of volume, of pageantry, of scene painting, but it is all economically done. The Victorian operatic ear, despite the efforts of Bernard Shaw, still preferred clarity and simplicity of form to "endless melody" and symphonic development, and the Victorian spirit that could enjoy passionate rhapsodizing in German and Italian expected a bit more restraint in English. These norms are as much linguistic as cultural; the English language sings differently from broad-voweled Italian and German. In a composer's ear, it must always be a matter of how the words sound, as Debussy would demonstrate in his exquisitely French *Pelléas*. Sullivan's "Englishness" may have been deemed old-fashioned by some, but in retrospect may as easily be heard as a foretaste of the post-Romantic modes of the coming century.

American opera lovers found, after the fully realized 1976 production in Houston, that for forty years we had possessed a national opera in Gershwin's *Porgy and Bess*. Like *Ivanhoe,* it is built of ballads, choruses, brief ensembles, and a succession of arioso passages linked by recitative, and its drama also creates a broad social picture through a wealth of characters, a description that equally applies to *Peter Grimes*. Even given a first-rate recording or a modern production unhampered by cumbersome scene changes, Sullivan's opera may still not assume the cultural position it might have earned had D'Oyly Carte's venture been more securely grounded in a developing repertory, but by reminding ourselves that *Ivanhoe* came at a time when opera composers everywhere were being challenged to reinvigorate the form, we may be able to appreciate better what the work truly is rather than lament what it is not. Its brilliant first run cannot have meant nothing, and many an undervalued continental opera has been known in our time to reach new and enthusiastic audiences. Sometimes it takes the passing of a century to see clearly a composer's lasting accomplishment.

I will close with a list of the operas by Sullivan's closest contemporaries that appeared after Verdi's penultimate masterpiece; note their variety and their varied fortunes in the international repertory.

> Chabrier (1841-1894): *Le Roi Malgré Lui* (Paris, 18 May 1887)
> Dvořák (1841-1904): *The Jacobin* (Prague, 12 February 1889)
> Massenet (1842-1912): *Esclarmonde* (Paris, 15 May 1889)
> Tchaikovsky (1840-1893):   *The Queen of Spades* (St. Petersburg, 19 December 1890)

Meanwhile, from his elders came Lalo's *Le Roi d'Ys* (1888) and Borodin's posthumous *Prince Igor* (1890) and from his juniors Catalani's *Loreley* (1890) and, of course, Mascagni's *Cavalleria Rusticana* (1890). This is noble company, and *Ivanhoe* is by no means unworthy of joining it.

THE COSTUMES

67

KÖNIGLICHE SCHAUSPIELHAUS BERLIN

LINDENOPER — C. FREYDANK, 1842

INTERIOR 1844

THE CRUSADER IN CONTEXT:

Operatic Versions of *Ivanhoe* and the Berlin production 1895/96

By Meinhard Saremba

This essay is based on a talk presented at the conference "Sullivanhoe – The Disinherited Opera" of the Sir Arthur Sullivan Society in Cirencester on 2nd October 2005.

Today people hardly ever read works by Walter Scott – at least in Germany. His output is mainly known to a wider audience through several films (*Ivanhoe* of 1952 or the *Quentin Durward* TV series of the 1970s). About two hundred years ago, Scott was extremely popular on the European mainland, especially in Germany. Goethe praised him in his conversations with Eckermann,[1] there was some correspondence between the two writers. The mutual esteem for the other's achievements is not surprising as Scott was inspired by Goethe's *Götz von Berlichingen* which he had translated himself. Even the highly critical Heinrich Heine remarked, despite some reservations, that Scott was "Britain's greatest author".[2] German translations and easily accessible editions of the 19th century reveal the popularity of the British author. For people learning the English language there were student editions of *Kenilworth* and *Ivanhoe*, for example – titles that appear prominently in Arthur Sullivan's output.[3] In the course of the 19th century, a certain Scott fashion became popular on the continent. How influential a writer he was is revealed in the fact that his ideas and his approach towards history and dramatic narration lived on in Italy in Carlo Manzoni whose most important novel *I promessi sposi*, first published in 1827, had a great influence on Verdi's operas and expressed his approach towards man in history and society. Why were people in central Europe fascinated by Scott? As well as being exciting literature, the books offered examples of how a solid country (and anything was more solid at that time than the many German or Italian states) defined its virtues and identity from the past.[4] This is where we find an important link between the achievements of Goethe and Scott: Byron dedicated a piece to Goethe as "the first of existing writers who has created the literature of his own country and illustrated that of Europe". What Goethe and Schiller had achieved in stage drama, Scott realized in the rising mass media of the 19th century: the novel. In Scott's historic novels, societies are no longer static organisms, but flexible phenomena with an interaction of the past, present and the future.[5] Scott's historic novels are no longer a continuation of a narrative tradition but a complimentary element to writing about history that blossomed in the 19th century.[6] The effectiveness and excitement of his works are revealed in the fact that for opera Scott is as important a writer as Shakespeare.[7]

Sullivan was surely acquainted with the popularity of Scott in Germany as he had studied in Leipzig, spoke German fluently and visited the country from time to time. His name was entered into German books on music and musicians in the early 1880s and he was hailed as the most promising English composer of choral and orchestral music, chamber works and comic opera. His popularity is emphasised by the fact that as late as 1910, the Swiss chocolate manufacturer Tobler offered advertising stamps with pictures of great composers. Sullivan was featured in this list among Gounod, Rossini, Handel, Mozart, Berlioz, Verdi, Puccini and others. Until the First World War, opera guides had mentioned his Scott opera *Ivanhoe*. Nevertheless one should not forget that in Germany from the late 1880s onwards, he was gradually reduced to the writer of comic opera only.[8] One should consider this important background information when focusing on his ambitious project of November 1895: a romantic opera on a grand scale had to undergo a serious test in Germany's capital. As early as the 4th January 1891, even before the world première, the manager of the Royal opera house in Berlin, Bolko Graf von Hochberg, addressed the terms of a contract in a telegram to Sullivan. As in most cases, Sullivan's diary entries reveal little emotion but one can be sure that – as his hero sings – like a mountain lark his spirit upwards sprang. Here was a great opportunity: If the Berlin performances were successful, this would open the doors to any opera houses in other cities and countries.

Forming of ideas

Taking into consideration the dramatic, historic and sociological potential of the *Ivanhoe* plot, this novel was a well-chosen starting point for the first opera to be presented in the newly built Royal English Opera House. From the beginning, Sullivan's ambitious opera project seemed to offer something for everybody. It is highly probable that he had this novel in mind at one of the rare occasions when he talked about concepts of his art – the big interview for the *San Francisco Chronicle* in July 1885. He intended to combine the best elements of all European styles in "an historical opera":

> The opera of the future is a compromise. I have thought and worked and toiled and dreamed of it. Not the French school, with gaudy and tinsel tunes, its lambent light and shades, its theatrical effects and clap-trap, not the Wagnerian school, with its sombreness and heavy ear-splitting airs, with its mysticism and unreal sentiment; not the Italian school, with its fantastic airs and *fioriture* and far-fetched effects. It is a compromise between these three – a sort of eclectic school, a selection of the merits of each one. I myself will make an attempt to produce a grand opera of this new school. Yes, it will be an historical work, and it is the dream of my life. I do not believe in operas based on gods and myths. That is the fault of the German school. It is metaphysical music – it is philosophy. What we want are plots which give rise to characters of flesh and blood, with human emotions and human passions. Music should speak to the heart, and not to the head.[9]

No wonder that the crusader for a new type of opera sympathized with the 12th century crusaders.

More evidence which proves that Sullivan had a realisation of *Ivanhoe* in mind at a very early stage of his career is that the "Jewish melody" in Rebecca's aria (Act 2, Scene 3) had been on his mind since his student days (September 1858- April 1861) when he visited the synagogue in Leipzig.[10] Rebecca became the only Jewish protagonist in Sullivan's output. His student days in Leipzig not only bore fruit concerning the development of his compositional skills, but also concerning the formation of his opinions. Sullivan was not the only artist who dreamt of a synthesis of different styles. Otto Nicolai (1810–1849) wrote in an article about "Italian and German Opera":

> In music we Germans can learn a lot from the Italians but, no doubt, they can learn even more from us. Concerning opera only a combination of the two schools can produce something that is a little closer to perfection, to absolute beauty. Mozart and Gluck knew this![11]

Those were attractive ideas and he produced several examples which illustrate them.[12] Is it possible that Sullivan read the article? Certainly, as it was published in 1837 in the *Neue Zeitschrift für Musik*, one of the best-known German music magazines, edited in Leipzig and founded by Robert Schumann.[13] He was acquainted with Nicolai's attempt at Shakespeare (*The Merry Wives of Windsor* from 1849) because it was part of the repertoire at the Leipzig opera house during his student years. Unfortunately Sullivan very rarely left comments on the origin of his ideas. On several occasions he mentioned Gioacchino Rossini (1792–1868) as one of his mentors.[14] Interestingly enough Nicolai and Rossini both tried to tackle *Ivanhoe* – a plot that does not come naturally to opera as it is too complicated and polygonal.

Another important name in the operatic career of *Ivanhoe* is Heinrich August Marschner (1795–1861). His opera *Der Templer und die Jüdin* – one of the most successful *Ivanhoe* versions of the 19th century – was part of the Leipzig repertoire where it was premièred thirty years before. Sullivan was still in Leipzig when Marschner died in Hannover on 14th February 1861, and Germany mourned the loss of one of its leading composers.[15] Apart from the fact that here another non-English composer seized a British topic with almost mythical qualities, something else in Marschner's approach to opera might have attracted Sullivan. In the 1820s there was a plan designed by Marschner to develop a concept of light opera, edited in volumes at a reasonable price so that members of the musical public, singing clubs or small music associations could perform them. This, according to Marschner, could help to develop the taste and the musical knowledge of the common man. Unfortunately Marschner could not realise this project due to financial difficulties, but at least Albert Lortzing brought comic opera in German to new peaks and half a century later. Sullivan realised something very similar to Marschner's concept. Sullivan's complaints in his 1888 Birmingham lecture that "Italian opera exclusively occupied the attention of the fashionable classes, and, like a great car of Juggernaut, overrode and crushed all efforts made on behalf of native music" is very similar to the German struggle for native opera to be free of the Italian and French influence. German romantic operas by Hoffmann, Weber or Marschner presented several examples of how to achieve this goal, and Sullivan summarised his stay in Leipzig thus: "Besides increasing and maturing my judgement of music it has taught me how good works ought to be done . . . ."

Competition from the European mainland

Apart from Sullivan, there were nine operatic versions of Scott's *Ivanhoe* in the course of the 19th century – none of them written by a British composer. While most versions enjoyed an ephemeral success[16] there were three composers with *Ivanhoe* versions that Sullivan wanted to surpass: Gioacchino Rossini's *Ivanhoé* (1826), Heinrich Marschner's *Der Templer und die Jüdin* (1829) and Otto Nicolai's *Il Templario* (1840).

To Rossini he owed his interest in the operatic stage and an enthusiasm to reach a wide audience. Sullivan was not reluctant to write opera as Nicolai was when he first came to Italy. Nicolai is like Sullivan in his ideas of combining different styles. A connection to the ordinary listener may go back to Marschner who, if anything, was probably closer to Sullivan's heart than Wagner. If Sullivan wanted to write a better *Ivanhoe* opera than they did – what were they like? As they were written for opera houses in France, Germany and Italy, they certainly contained elements of the "schools" mentioned above by Sullivan.

Rossini's *Ivanhoé* is a *pastiche*, that is a "medley" arranged in collaboration with another composer or editor based on previous compositions.[17] Rossini had always wanted to compose for the French stage, especially for "L'Opéra": the 19th century "operatic Hollywood". As a master of showmanship, he knew how to arouse curiosity: Rossini wanted to introduce himself to the Paris audience *before* he offered his French opera *Le Siège de Corinthe* to L'Opéra which was a revision of *Maometto II*. Rossini's *Ivanhoé* opened at the Théatre de L'Odéon[18] on 15th September 1826, three weeks before *Siège* and seven years after the novel. Rossini worked together with Antonio Pacini, who was born in Naples and had lived in Paris since 1804. He worked as a music publisher as well as author of operas and romances, but he is not a relative of the Italian composer Giovanni Pacini who wrote his own version of *Ivanhoe* in 1832. *Ivanhoé* with Rossini's music in Antonio Pacini's arrangement became the only *Ivanhoe* opera that Scott himself saw on stage. "In the evening at the Odéon, where we saw *Ivanhoe*", he remembered in his *Journal*: "It was superbly got up, the Norman soldiers wearing pointed helmets and what resembles much hauberks of mail, which looked very well. The number of the attendants, and the skill with which they were moved and grouped on the stage, were well worthy of notice. It was an opera, and of course the story greatly mangled and the dialogue in a great part nonsense."[19] Scott did not mention the music at all, which probably didn't impress him.

Ivanhoé is an "opéra comique" on a French libretto, that is an opera with music *and* dialogue. It was often said that Rossini was not involved in creating this pasticcio but the fanfares that precede the third act finale are so overtly reminiscent of the famous fanfares in the last section of the *William Tell* overture (written three years later) that Pacini would not have gained access to this music without Rossini's collaboration.[20] Rossini supported and probably advised Pacini in plundering his own works.[21] In *Ivanhoé* the origins of the numbers are sometimes surprising [see table II] since the sources include *opera buffa* as well as *opera seria*. As a result, the music can hardly offer any individual characterisation. To make the adaptation easier, the original key remains in most cases, the music is shortened and the original melodic lines are simplified. A striking example is the metamorphosis of a comic scene that is turned into a dramatic one in Ismael's aria in the first act. It is based on Don Magnifico's aria "Sia qualunque delle figlie" from the second act of *La Cenerentola*. In the Cinderella opera, Don Magnifico tells his daughters in *parlando* style that when one of them soon ascends the throne, she should not abandon the magnificent papa. As there are no comic elements in Rossini's French *Ivanhoé*, the music has to undergo a substantial transformation to suit the occasion: Ismael, a Muslim (!) – who is none other than Scott's Isaac of York – sings about Bois-Guilbert and what an unpleasant fellow he is. In the second and third verses he describes how he and his daughter Leila tried to escape the Templar. Certainly Don Magnifico's passages in *falsetto* (typically used in comic works) are eliminated, a chorus is added in order to support a dramatic crescendo and some lively passages of violins in the second verse are performed by clarinets.

The change of names reveals a disrespectful exploitation of Scott's novel.[22] Probably the authors feared that people could object to Jews on the stage. Other interventions in the plot led to decisive departures from the original story as in some other versions [see table I].[23] Nevertheless Rossini's concoction remained quite successful and was also produced in London in 1829 as *The Maid of Judah or The Knight Templars* (followed by performances in Dublin, New York, and Philadelphia).[24]

When an Italian composer was able to succeed in France – why not a German composer in Italy? After his first Italian opera *Enrico II* had resulted in a lukewarm reaction in Triest in 1839, Otto Nicolai[25] received an excellent reception for *Il Templario* in Turin in 1840. His *Ivanhoe* version, which switched the emphasis to the villain, was repeated many times in Italy and Europe. *Il Templario* is a through-composed "number" opera with *recitativo secco*.[26] As in Rossini's version the complex structure of the novel is simplified to some essential elements [see table I]: the many threads of the plot and the number of people are reduced and the music includes several 19th century Italian opera stereotype devices such as the conventional *andante-stretta* aria type. [see table IV]. The melodic model goes back to Bellini, but some dramatic effects hint at Donizetti's influence. Some choral parts may be influenced by Rossini's *William Tell*. People praised the scoring for the orchestra which towered high above the ordinary level of the mass production of Italian opera. [see table V]

Nevertheless this work could not match the success of Marschner's *Der Templer und die Jüdin* (*The Templar and the Jewess*) which became his most popular opera up to the early 20th century. Despite this fact, *Der Templer* is overshadowed today by much better known works such as *Hans Heiling* or *Der Vampyr*. Although Marschner's operatic output is in some respect a forerunner of Wagner, Marschner did not represent the German school that Sullivan had in mind in his famous interview. Certainly the format of Marschner's ensemble influenced Wagner and the statement that the finale of *Der Templer und die Jüdin* was a forerunner of the trial scene in *Lohengrin* (although Marschner requires two scenes until the saviour comes, whereas Wagner is more concise and dramatic) is justified. Marschner, who also worked as a conductor, further developed the demonic, dramatic baritone part in German opera and – like Wagner – he was sometimes accused of ruining singers' voices. His development from *Singspiel* to romantic opera shows a gradual replacement of individual solo song by recitative or scene and aria and an increase of ensemble numbers over solo pieces. Marschner's stage work represents the peak of German romantic opera. Wagner simply had to follow the paths created by Marschner and Weber.

Der Templer und die Jüdin was premièred on 22nd December 1829, while Marschner was Kapellmeister in Leipzig (1827-1830). As the original version was considered to be too long – there were several complaints about too much dialogue – Marschner revised the opera. After an enormous success it was staged all over Europe (even in London in 1840 and New York in 1872), although each theatre seemed to have developed its own adaptation from the quarry of eighteen musical numbers with text, which added up to a length of about four hours.[27] In the vein of the better-known opera *Der Freischütz* by Weber, it features a structure of dialogue and music [see table III]. The Ashby scene is omitted and – as the title suggests – the conflict between Rebecca and Sir Brian is central as it is in all *Ivanhoe* operas. Marschner's version is not only based on Scott but also on popular plays after Scott's *Ivanhoe*: The librettist W.A. Wohlbrück plundered *Das Gericht der Templer* by Johann Reinhold Lenz (1778-1854)[28] and *Der Löwe von Kurdistan* (1827) by Joseph Freiherr von Auffenberg (after Scott's *Talisman*).[29]

73

Der Templer und die Jüdin.

Große romantische Oper in drei Acten.

Text nach Walter Scott's Roman „Ivanhoe"
frei bearbeitet von
W. A. Wohlbrück.
Musik
von
Heinrich Marschner.

Klavierauszug mit Text, Recitativen und Dialog.

Nach der Partitur berichtigt und neu bearbeitet
von
Richard Kleinmichel.

In dieser Ausgabe Eigenthum des Verlages für alle Länder
Aufführungsrecht vorbehalten.

UNIVERSAL-EDITION
AKTIENGESELLSCHAFT
WIEN-LEIPZIG

HEINRICH MARSCHNER 1795-1861

OTTO NICOLAI 1810-1849

This opera already expanded the resources of the *Singspiel* with more complex ensemble numbers; the influence on Sullivan's opera may be – in contrast to all other *Ivanhoe* operas – that there is a mixture of comic and dramatic scenes. This certainly highlights Marschner's concept of writing operas for the people, not especially for the establishment or connoisseurs. Wagner criticized Marschner because everything in his work is on a "small scale" and reveals "a lack of an overall effect".[30] Nevertheless he praises the grand aria of the Templar "Mich zu verschmähen? Stolze, Undankbare!" because of its "volcano-like passion which makes it a creation of great originality in invention and an ingenious melodic invention."[31]

Due to the rise of the Wagnerian music drama in the second half of the 19th century, it is not surprising that audiences lost the liking for Marschner. His biggest success, *Der Templer und die Jüdin*, suffers from bad timing, for example with two entertaining songs for the fool Wamba and the monk respectively. There is another unnecessary repetition when the Templar threatens Rebecca twice. The proportions of the work are not well-balanced because of sometimes rather short musical numbers between extensive dialogues and lengthy finales. In the theatrical practice of the 19th century and later, people tried to improve the work; the most prominent example may be Pfitzner's revision of the trial by ordeal against Rebecca, when he combined the original two scenes (Acts II/3 and III/3) into one. If one considers a major cut by Marschner himself – the scene in De Bracy's castle – then there is the same structure as in Sullivan/Sturgis: Three acts with three scenes (containing different aspects and plotting). Where Sullivan however catches the *couleur locale*[32] within one minute in his prelude, Marschner writes a ten minute overture with only a few of the major tunes.[33] The best known scene and the only vocal number of Marschner's opera that was recorded later became Rebecca's "Preghiera" in act 3.[34] This song with its accompaniment of harp, horns, strings and basses is an impressive piece, but impersonal compared to Sullivan's aria which contains an element of Leipzig synagogue music. It hardly seemed probable that a German composer of the 19th century would use elements of Jewish music in the sympathetic way Sullivan had.[35] Scott's and Sullivan's hero Ivanhoe is hardly relevant in Marschner's arrangement of the plot in which, like the swan knight, he suddenly appears almost from nowhere.

Dealing with complexity

Almost all the operatic versions seem to lead to the conclusion that *Ivanhoe* is not suited for the operatic stage. Works such as *Il Templario* or *Der Templer und die Jüdin* only dramatised part of the plot. In fact, all versions were more or less abridged in order to reduce the complexity of the novel. In some cases, Ivanhoe was not regarded as an especially interesting hero since he remains too passive; consequently, the title was often changed as were, at least sometimes, the names of the characters. Ivanhoe mainly appears as the saviour close to the end which in some versions gives him a somewhat baroque *Deus ex machina* function. Scott's *Ivanhoe*, however, remained so dramatic a plot that it would have been a pity to lose it to the operatic stage. It was a rather brave enterprise when – half a century after Nicolai's *Il Templario*, 25 years after Pisani's *Rebecca* and 10 years after Castegnier's *Rébecca* – Arthur Sullivan and Julian Sturgis pursued a new attempt.

Sullivan and Sturgis presented the first opera version in which Ivanhoe was seen as the catalyst of the action: the character who is in touch with all the other "threads" and elements of the story – in other words, the "nucleus". No doubt that the Templar is one of the most fascinating protagonists. However, in order to do justice to the complex story, one has to find a solution to the crucial problem of the Rowena – Ivanhoe – Rebecca relationship. This is not easy because even Scott's Rowena was not regarded as a convincing character. For the ordinary reader and spectator the question remained: Why should the saviour-hero not marry the girl he saved? (Thackeray was so occupied with this that he even left a sequel to *Ivanhoe*, entitled *Rebecca and Rowena*, in which Rowena dies so that Ivanhoe and Rebecca can become a couple.) Some of the solutions offered were quite unsatisfactory. Rossini did not know what to do with Rowena at all and in his pastiche the role is omitted altogether. The surprise at the end is that Leila, a muslim – originally Scott's Rebecca – turns out to be Edith, daughter of Olric, the last descendant of the Saxon kings. In Giovanni Pacini's *Ivanhoe* (1832) Rowena is Ivanhoe's sister. For Marschner, Rowena remains unimportant; at the end Cedric gives permission for the marriage but Rebecca, who does not withdraw with her father, replies to the king that she has received reward enough in having Ivanhoe fight for her. In Nicolai's opera Rebecca declares her love for Ivanhoe before all (in Scott her pride precludes these emotions). Ivanhoe answers that if she loves him she must remain silent and in a typical Italian opera finale, Rebecca faints into her father's arms whereas Rowena remains silent.

Sullivan's version enhances Rowena's position by additional material in order to create a credible character. For example in Act 2 Scene 2, De Bracy tells Rowena that Ivanhoe will live if she becomes his bride. Rowena implores him to save Ivanhoe, which is not in the novel but strengthens her character. Sullivan discovers the true dramatic potential of the plot: a man and two women who could be *his* – could there be any more emotional conflict? Neither should we forget Sir Brian de Bois-Guilbert, who is both a man evil enough to threaten Rebecca *and* a lover who later (against his will) is forced by the Grand Master of the Templars to destroy the person he loves - the same Rebecca - in an ordeal. He is overcome by his inner conflicts which lead to the strange heart-attack ending in Sullivan's opera as well as in the novel.

Sullivan is a master of creating atmosphere and exploring the nature of the characters. Nevertheless, doubts remain whether he really did full justice to the inner conflicts of the protagonists. Where Rossini, Nicolai and Marschner were restricted by the boundaries of their national type of opera, Sullivan declared that he wanted to establish "a compromise between these three – a sort of eclectic school, a selection of the merits of each one." The result was a number opera with long passages of through-composed scenes with the established standards of character types (tenor hero, soprano heroines, baritone villain, bass for comic and royal roles). At least in the 20th century the term "eclectic" achieved a negative connotation. Wasn't it destined to extinction in a time when art had to be revolutionary and progressive? The new century also saw other developments where the musical became the stage mass entertainment and the large operatic scores were written for the movies. An opera that seems to be based on Sullivan's principles is Gershwin's *Porgy and Bess*, in which the composer uses elements from all possible sources in order to express the appropriate emotion.[36]

Sullivan's opera became the most complex and advanced *Ivanhoe* opera of 19th century. To some extent it was even up to the standards of 1890s and beyond: Due to the fragmentation of the plot into nine scenes, it is reminiscent of a video–clip technique compared to *Parsifal* – which will make *Ivanhoe* a challenge for modern stages.[37] The short orchestral introduction (as in Verdi's late operas there is no long overture) and some impressionistic elements with the delicacy of the French orchestral style, clearly establishes that the orchestra is one of the opera's leading characters. Sullivan's vocal writing explores the natural speech rhythm which became important for many opera composers later. With its demands on the staging and the mixture of drama and entertainment, *Ivanhoe* is closer to *The Force of Destiny* than *Aida*. In Rossini's and Nicolai's versions as in others of the French/Italian approach, there are no comic elements. This may lead to the conclusion that established opera nations don't need to please everybody and distinguish strictly between *opera seria* and *opera buffa*. Marschner and Sullivan are urged by a similar motivation as representatives not of established but of up-and-coming, aspiring opera countries: the "Shakespearian" approach of trying to satisfy different expectations and audiences.

Some of the most prominent aspects of the "Sullivan touch" in the music are the melodic invention, the sure-footed approach of creating atmosphere as well as the brilliant instrumentation and word-setting. *Ivanhoe* is an episodic opera like Mussorgski's *Boris Godunov* or *Chovanchtshina*, but it does not have their gloomy atmosphere. It is a democratic opera which takes into consideration the development of musical audiences in 19th century. In addition, the contrasting elements and casting make it a perfect ensemble opera. With the fusion of diverse elements in *Ivanhoe*, Sullivan had not written an English opera but rather, a European one.

The crucial test ahead

With the most complex of all *Ivanhoe* operas, Sullivan tried his luck in the country where he had learnt his trade: Germany. The idea to introduce the new work to Berlin was broached before the London première on 31st January 1891. The mainly favourable reactions were spread in Germany where papers reported "a sweeping success"[38] – a verdict on the music based on London reviews. The plan to perform the new opera in Berlin may have its roots in the relationships between the royal houses in Berlin and London. *Ivanhoe* operas seem to lend themselves to royal dedications. Interestingly enough, in connection with *Ivanhoe* Sullivan and Marschner both dedicated works to British rulers: Sullivan his 1891 opera to Queen Victoria – the mother of the English-born Prussian Queen and Empress Vicky and grand-mother to the Emperor Wilhelm II – and Marschner an overture surrounding the opera to King George IV of England.[39] Nicolai's opera was dedicated to the wife of the King of Sardinia.[40] In Berlin it was regarded as a sort of "duty" of the Königliche Schauspiele (Royal Drama) to perform Sullivan's work. If there had been some correspondence which could prove that the performances took place due to the order of the Kaiser – which one can sometimes read in the press – then none of it remained. What we can be sure of is this: In the 1890s the theatre that is now the Staatsoper Unter den Linden in Berlin was officially called Die Königlichen Schauspiele as an institution (since 1817) which consisted of the Schauspielhaus and the opera house (which became Staatsoper in 1918 after the Kaiser had abdicated). Due to its status there was a certain imperial influence and in a speech the Emperor mentioned how pleased he was that the theatre acknowledged the things he wanted to see on stage.[41]

The German première of *Ivanhoe* was scheduled for an earlier date than 1895. After Bolko Graf von Hochberg, manager of the Königliche Schauspiele, had approached Sullivan for the terms of a contract in a telegram dated 4 January 1891 – one month before the première – Sullivan travelled to Berlin in November 1893 to prepare the performances. He stayed in Berlin for eleven days from Thursday, 23 November to Monday, 4 December 1893. Most of the time the weather was "wet and nasty" with a late change on 2 December 1893: "Snow, hard frost, though sunshine – what a change!"[42] According to his diaries, Sullivan discussed the sets and some cuts[43] with Friedrich Brandt, the chief machinist of the opera house. He went through the score with the conductor Carl Muck, a "nice little man", and met members of the cast. Sullivan was especially fond of the 28-year old Ida Hiedler who was to sing Rebecca, a "pleasant, intelligent girl", whom he met three times.

Apart from seeing some of his own works in Berlin,[44] Sullivan went to performances at the Königlichen Schauspiele in order to get an impression of the artistic standards. After Mozart's *Idomeneo* and *The Abduction from the Seraglio* on 25 November he came to the conclusion: "Frau Herzog (Constanze) brilliant high voice, sings very well, good for Rowena; Lieban small but useful tenor (De Bracy); Mädlinger as Selim very good – Friar Tuck or Cedric . . ." A performance of Meyerbeer's *L'Africaine* on 28 November 1893 under Josef Sucher was "abominable, accents coarse and loud, stage band and orchestra not together". He was very much impressed by a new piece, *Mara* by Ferdinand Hummel, which had its world première on 11 October 1893. Sullivan saw the work about seven weeks later. The production took place under the baton of Carl Muck with Mrs Pierson in the title role. One might suspect that Sullivan did not realise what he entered into when he dared to criticise the lead: "Pierson would not do for Rebecca". Unfortunately the singer Bertha Pierson was the wife of Count Hochberg's private secretary, Henry Pierson. An unpleasant incident occurred on 29th November 1893: "Wrote to Pierson (about his wife and Rebecca) and Hochberg (with cast) when I . . . sending them, in came Pierson, so I explained why I could not invite Mad. Pierson to sing Rebecca (gave him my letter) . . ." Was Sullivan fool-hardy, brave, honest or did he simply underestimate the situation? By some people Pierson was supposed to be very influential in the hierarchy of the opera house, a sort of grey eminence behind Hochberg. Although Sullivan was confident when "Hochberg . . . proposes that 'Ivanhoe' should come out in January or early February" it took another two years until the work was finally performed. Was this due to insulting Pierson's wife?

This did not remain the only missed opportunity on his visit to Berlin. Sullivan contacted the librettist of *Mara*, the new opera about which he was so enthusiastic: "Splendidly dramatic plot – music pretentious rubbish and 'Klangeffect' ugly and colourless." Mara's story[45] is so totally different from *Ivanhoe*'s that it, or something similar in that vein would have been a great challenge for Sullivan. It is highly interesting to discover in the diaries that "(Axel) Delmar (author of *Mara*) called to see me about a book". Unfortunately the chance for an inspiring collaboration vanished into obscurity.

Phoenix from the ashes

In total it took more than four years, almost five, until the German première of *Ivanhoe* was realised. This was not necessarily worrying or unusual. In comparison, it took three years after the première of Verdi's *Otello* in 1887, until the first new Verdi opera after 16 years saw the Berlin stage on 1st February 1890 (conducted by Josef Sucher, whose artistic capabilities Sullivan did not appreciate, and with Eloi Sylva and Paul Bulss – the forthcoming male leads for *Ivanhoe*).

Why did Sullivan's *Ivanhoe* arrive so late on the Berlin stage? A possible intrigue by Pierson – due to the insult of refusing his wife – remains speculation. Casting the work cannot have been a problem as German opera houses at that time had a regular ensemble for meeting all necessary demands. There are, however, other practical reasons. First of all a translation was necessary since in those days all operas were performed in the mother-tongue of the country. In order to cope with the great scenic demands, the theatre ordered completely new sets. This was not common because theatre companies normally used manufactured standard sets and paintings for their general demand: a forest, a chamber, a castle etc. from specialized companies that provided sets for the many theatres in Germany. The high cost for new sets made it seem rather likely that the management used the well-meaning of the Emperor towards *Ivanhoe* to order new sets which could be used for something else later (as suggested by some of the reviewers).[46]

The paintings for the stage scenery and backgrounds were done by different artists and manufacturers: Eugen Quaglio (who also designed the sets for *Der Mikado* in a 1900 production), Mr. Mettenleiter, Georg Hartwig, Mr. Wagner, Mr. Bukacz – all names were especially mentioned on the playbill for later performances as if the management tried to attract people with new sets, not with the work itself (programme booklets as we know them today were not developed until the late 1920s). In November 1893 Sullivan had to make cuts of about 24 minutes.[47] The Berlin production had four acts with seven scenes instead of three acts with three scenes. There was a tendency to make the action move faster. Scenes between King Richard and Friar Tuck (Act II/1) were probably regarded as being non-dramatic; and there is also a cut in Act III/2 when the melody of the King's song is repeated – the song was also unsuccessful and the theatre people probably did not like it and regarded the scene as dramatically weak. A cut of two minutes in Act II/2 reduces the role of Rowena because people could not see De Bracy declaring his love for her and she is also deprived of her lengthy duet with Ivanhoe in Act III/2 when Isaac immediately appears.

The story became concentrated on Rebecca and the father-son conflict. In Act II/3, cuts deprive the action of Ulrica's sinister reply to the suffering girl. When Rebecca asks "Is there no way to safety?", Ulrica does not answer: "No way but through the gates of death . . ." but goes on immediately with "Not even the presence of the mother of god can save thee". Even the scene that is central to all *Ivanhoe* operas – the confrontation of the Jewish girl with the menacing Templar – is not spared: There is a huge cut in Act II/3 when Rebecca threatens to leap down the castle wall to death and Sir Brian declares his love for her and tells her how – as the Head of the Order – he can live with her. A Christian loves a Jewess passionately – probably too much of a good thing for audiences who mainly shared Wagner's sentiments.[48] Similar reasons may have been behind the cuts of the Ivanhoe – Rebecca scene (Act III/1) where the hero is not allowed to have a tender scene with a Jewess and of Act III/3 where they are not interested in self-defence of a Jewess ("I am innocent etc."). In general, one might say that in musical terms, the cuts are very cleverly done. They mainly apply to scenes where the soloists are accompanied by only a few orchestral chords or where Christians declare their love or sympathy for a Jewess too openly. [Whether the same cuts were used for the Carl Rosa Company's four-act version of *Ivanhoe* is not quite clear: On 19 December 1893, after the visit to Berlin, Sullivan met Dr Bridge concerning the Carl Rosa production. This project could not be realized until 14 Feb 1895 in Liverpool (scenery: W.F. Robson; conductor: Claude Jaquinot).]

Everything seemed to be prepared for the German première early in 1894. The problems discussed above may explain why it took place three years after the London production (a common time span in those days). According to the diary, the cast was not quite clear. It is also surprising that Sullivan mentioned Friedrich Brandt as "chief machinist" whereas the Ober-Regisseur der Oper (head producer) Carl Tetzlaff was finally responsible for the production. Probably an accident led to the postponement of the first night. In November 1895 the *Berliner Tageblatt* reminded its readers that *Ivanhoe* was "persecuted by misfortune: Last year (1894) the opera was prepared up to the dress rehearsal when the composer Sullivan fell down the stairs, hurt his foot just at the moment when he wanted to travel to Berlin . . . As a result of his request, the performance was postponed . . . on the 5th of this month the royal opera singer Miss Hiedler, who will sing the important role of Rebecca, slipped on the stairs in Dresden where she sang in concerts and hurt her knee. . . . ." In his diaries Sullivan did not mention these incidents and there are no telegrams or letters by the composer in Hochberg's papers and correspondence.[49] If an accident happened, why should they put aside all the energy and efforts that they had put into the preparation and postpone it for one and a half years when they would have to study the parts again? Were they waiting for a better occasion or were they not especially keen on channelling energy into a demanding project that was imposed upon them? Between March and May 1894 the Königlichen Schauspiele saw several Berlin or German premières: *I Medici* by Leoncavallo, a new and rising star of opera world and a favourite of the Emperor, on 17 February 1894 (with the *Ivanhoe* leads Sylva and Bulss in the cast) – a work that was premièred in the previous year. Also one year after world première there was Verdi's last opera *"Falstaff* on 6 March 1894 and Smetana's *The Bartered Bride* in May. Later followed a new, demanding production of *Der Prophet* on 4 October 1894 and a new *Rienzi* on 23 March 1895, both with the tenor Eloi Sylva in the title role. The 4th May 1895 saw the world première of Kienzl's *Der Evangelimann* (*The Evangelist*) with Sylva and Bulss.

Taking into consideration a wide-spread practice at opera houses the "accident" was probably just an excuse because the sets were not finished in time or all these other new works may have been more promising for the management. There may have been a certain reluctance, even unwillingness to realise the project. *The Neue Berliner Musikzeitung* remarked: "The management of the Hofoper is up to a nice business trick: They announce shabby operatic trousers, worn-out in rehearsals for years, which are embarrassing for them and in which up to now they have not dared to present themselves to the public with the following puffing . . ." (21 November 1895). In the meantime the fuss about *Ivanhoe* had become grotesque for some observers. In a preliminary report the *Berliner Tageblatt*, which was the most important newspaper of the capital at that time, stated: "Tomorrow, on Tuesday, *Ivanhoe* will be performed at the Royal Opera House: Finally!, say the serious people; Already?, the ironic; Who knows!?, the superstitious . . ." (25 November 1895).

Good preparation is all

If some people had not taken Sullivan's *Ivanhoe* seriously, the preparation for the German première would have been sloppy. There were, however, many experienced and committed people involved. Although some artists complained about the "office-like atmosphere" and "red-tape Prussian style" at the opera house where too many orders and devotion to fulfil the requirements left little room for art and imagination, many of them praised the high-quality orchestra, the excellent chorus, some very good soloists.[50] The German translation[51] of Sturgis' libretto lay in the hands of the cosmopolitan Hugo Wittmann (1839–1923).[52] Although he is not always accurate concerning the rhyme structure in the arias and duets, he did a good job with his solid, reliable German version of *Ivanhoe* which is not better but by no means worse than other translations of that time. The meaning of the text is conveyed very well and Wittmann shows a good sense for the musical demands when he is very careful with the *sound* of words.[53] A major problem with opera translations is that there are a lot of short words in the English language which require more syllables in German, for example: "France" which becomes "Frank – reich". Wittman therefore sometimes is, and has to be, flexible with the rhythm and note lengths especially when the contents of a statement is more important than musical necessities: As in Act 1, Scene 3 where we find the only historic quotation in the libretto when a messenger presents a letter to Prince John. In this situation John sings:

English: "'Tis from our Royal brother, Louis of France: (10 syllables)
Look for thyself! The devil has broken loose!'" (11)

German: "Von unserem Freunde Ludwig, König von Frankreich: (13 syllables)
"Nimm Dich in Acht, der Teufel ist wieder frei!'" (11)

A crucial question for opera translation remains: If *Ivanhoe* had been a success, are there any lines that would have had the chance of becoming "classical", even "quotable"? Wittmann's translation has this quality with Rowena's "O Mond wie dein Licht dem Silber gleich, erstrahlt in stiller Ruh'!", Ivanhoe's "Gleich einer Lerche zieht's mich himmelwärts!", Sir Brian's "Wirb um die Kalte, bis das Eis zerschmilzt", Rowena's "Herr, Gott Jehova, stehe du mir bei" or Tuck's "Der Wind bläst eisig übers Moor" – a potential hit song.[54] Unfortunately these arias were never recorded in the 1920s, 30s, 40s or 50s, the prime time of opera recordings in German.

Wanting to be equal to the occasion

Concerning the casting, the management did everything to do themselves proud.[55] Some of the ensemble members became famous later and their achievements are documented on records. The most prominent name of the cast is Carl Muck (1859– 1940), who became a popular Wagner conductor. He, too, had studied in Leipzig but twenty years after Sullivan. From 1892 to 1912 Muck was Hofkapellmeister at the opera of the Königliche Schauspiele in Berlin, then he went to the Boston Symphony Orchestra where he stayed between 1912 and 1915. Later he worked for the Hamburger Philharmonie, and in Munich, Amsterdam, London, Vienna and Bayreuth, where he conducted all *Parsifal* performances between 1901 and 1930. In the 1920s, when Toscanini came to Bayreuth, Muck was one of the group who supported the "Bayreuth for Germans only" attitude. "Muck conducting very satisfactorily", Sullivan remarked in diaries after an *Ivanhoe* rehearsal.

The Belgian tenor Eloi Sylva (1843–1919) was a pupil of Gilbert Duprez in Brussels. Aged 52 when he performed Ivanhoe, Sylva was still one of the leading artists for dramatic tenor roles in French and Italian opera although he was not very attractive due to his short legs.[56] He is said to have a powerful, robust voice – no wonder that he sang Canio one day before an *Ivanhoe* performance; he even sang the Ivanhoe role twice within two days. According to Count Hochberg, Sylva was "a first-rate dramatic tenor – with his phenomenal voice which possesses an extraordinary stamina he remains a reliable pillar for the repertoire."[57]

To some extent this also goes for Paul Bulss (1842–1902), who as a descendant of a Junker's estate was the only "nobleman" of the cast and worthy of singing the Templar Knight. He was also said to be arrogant, which suits the role. He performed almost the complete standard repertoire of German and Italian opera but featured also as a concert singer, for example with the solo in the first night of Mahler's *Des Knaben Wunderhorn*.[58] It his highly possible that the year 1895 was the beginning of the end of his powers as the files show that he had to cancel several performances due to hoarseness or illness, among them an *Ivanhoe* performance. In March 1900 a letter of Count Hochberg's pen reveals that the management was no longer willing to renew the expiring contract, at least "not if Bulss is not willing to reduce his demands".[59]

Concerning the role of Rowena, Sullivan succeeded and Bertha Pierson did not sing it but Adrienne Weitz (1865 – after 1920), a 30-year-old soprano from Hannover.[60] According to Count Hochberg he appreciated her achievements although her "physical and vocal powers were limited" so she could not be used within the ensemble in a flexible way.[61]

Sullivan's favourite Ida Hiedler (1867–1932) must have been ideal for Rebecca. Count Hochberg engaged the 28-year-old daughter of a Viennese imperial official straight from the Conservatoire. She developed from lyrical roles to the challenging dramatic heroines.[62] In Count Hochberg's letters, there is nothing but praise about this artist who "fulfilled the tasks she had to do with a never tiring diligence and a restless passion", not to forget her "brilliant voice and looks that are very much to her advantage".[63]

King Richard the Lionheart was sung by Emil Stammer (1858–1926), a bass who had started his career as an actor before he turned to opera.[64] At the age of 37 he was much younger than the other male leads. Franz Krolop (1839–1897), who sang Friar Tuck, was an artist with whom Sullivan had worked eight years earlier. Krolop sang the bass role in two performances of *Die Goldene Legende* in Berlin in 1887 when Sullivan conducted. He was a highly appreciated member of the ensemble and his unexpected death during an emergency operation after a performance was a major loss for the opera house.[65] The cast member best documented on recordings was Marie Goetze (1865–1922), the 30-year-old Ulrica. A few years later she sang Katisha when *Der Mikado* was performed at the opera house of the Königliche Schauspiele in June 1900. She had a trashy novel-like career when as a daughter of a Prussian government official she had to fight for her dream to become an opera singer – in the years to come she was very much in demand between Berlin and New York for all the signigficant roles of her repertoire.[66]

The great opportunity

Looking at the cast list on paper, one might say that the initial position for the German première of *Ivanhoe* was ideal – Sullivan virtually had the best artists who were available in Germany. The first night eventually took place on 26 November 1895. All performances were scheduled from from 7:30 to after 10:30. There was an interval after the third act (that is Act III/1 of the London version, with the Ivanhoe-Rebecca duet and where the Templar drags the Jewish girl away). Berlin had special prices for the first night (about one third higher than usual whereas there were no extra prices for other first nights, world premières or big Wagner operas). This might have been due to the expensive new sets;[67] in the normal repertoire the usual prices for *Ivanhoe* remained – probably to attract more people to come. There were text booklets available at the price of 50 Pfennigs (this was half of the price for the standing-room, which was one Mark). The German libretto survived but unfortunately neither performance material nor sketches of the costume design or the scenery exist.[68] The German audience was a critical and crucial test for the composer. A success might have opened

IDA HIEDLER 1867-1932

ELOI SILVA 1843-1919

PAUL BULSS 1842-1902

BOLKO VON HOCHBERG 1843-1926

Königliche 🦅 Schauspiele.

Opernhaus.

Dienstag, den 26. November 1895.

Mit aufgehobenem Abonnement. Zum ersten Mal:

Ivanhoe.

Romantische Oper in 4 Akten von Arthur Sullivan.
Nach Walther Scott's gleichnamigem Roman bearbeitet von Julian
Sturgis, deutsch von H. Wittmann
In Scene gesetzt vom Ober-Regisseur Tetzlaff
Dirigent: Kapellmeister Dr. Muck.

Richard Löwenherz, König von England, verkleidet als schwarzer Ritter	Herr Stammer.
Prinz Johann, sein Bruder	Herr Fränkel.
Cedric der Sachse, Herr auf Rotherwood	Herr Schmidt.
Wilfried von Ivanhoe, sein verstoßener Sohn, als Pilger verkleidet	Herr Sylva.
Lady Rowena sein Mündel	Fräul. Weitz.
Lucas de Beaumanoir, Großmeister } des Templer-Ordens	Herr Mödlinger.
Brian de Bois Guilbert, Comthur } des Templer-Ordens	Herr Bulß.
Maurice de Bracy, ein normannischer Ritter	Herr Philipp.
Bruder Tuck, der Einsiedler von Copmanhurst	Herr Krolop.
Locksley, Anführer der Geächteten	Herr Sommer.
Isaak von York, ein Jude	Herr Krasa.
Rebecca, seine Tochter	Fräul. Hiedler.
Ulrica	Frau Goetze.
Wamba, Narr } in Cedrics Diensten	Herr Müller.
Oswald, Haushofmeister } in Cedrics Diensten	Herr Quaritsch.
Ein Thürhüter Cedrics	Herr Alma.
Turnier-Herolde	Herren Selle, Sillge, Grün, Winkler.

Sächsische und normannische Ritter, Knappen, Edelknaben und Damen.
Mannen und Gesinde Cedrics. Tempelritter und Knappen. Reisige.
Geächtete. Landleute und Volk.
Ort der Handlung: England. Zeit: Gegen Ende des 12. Jahrhunderts

Nach dem 3. Akt findet eine längere Pause statt.

Der Billet-Verkauf findet im Opern- und Schauspielhause täglich
für alle angekündigten Vorstellungen statt.

Der Billet-Verkauf findet statt:	Sonn- und Festtage.	Wochentage.
Auf Meldungen reservirte Billets mit 50 Pf. Bestellgeld	9—10 Uhr.	9—10 Uhr.
Nicht reservirte Billets	12—1/2 2 „	10½„ — 1

Bei Rückgabe der Billets in Folge Wegfalls oder Abänderung der Vorstellung
wird auch das Bestellgeld zurückgezahlt.

Die Billet-Inhaber werden ersucht, vor dem Betreten des Zu-
schauerraumes den Coupon vom Billet trennen zu lassen. Derselbe ist
bis zum Schlusse der Vorstellung als Legitimation aufzubewahren.

Die im Königlichen Opernhause und im Königlichen Schauspielhause
gefundenen Gegenstände sind durch die Verlierer von der Hauspolizei-
Inspection im Opernhaus resp. Schauspielhaus **innerhalb 4 Wochen**
abzufordern.

Mittwoch: Der Evangelimann. — Phantasien im Bremer
Rathskeller.

Kassen-Eröffnung 6½ Uhr. Anfang 7½ Uhr. Ende nach 10½ Uhr.

the doors of opera houses world-wide. According to the playbills, twelve performances were planned for the 1895/96 season. Finally, only ten took place due to the illness of singers.[69] The cancelled performances were never rescheduled nor did *Ivanhoe* remain in the repertoire of the coming years.

Sullivan stayed in snowy Berlin from Tuesday, 12 November to Wednesday, 27 November 1895, eleven days for attending the rehearsals and the first performance. He suffered from stomach problems which might have contributed to his uneven temper at the beginning of his stay. According to his diaries, he was first annoyed about some "unsatisfactory things in scenery" but he "put them right" after "struggles with Brandt, but got my way" (14 November 1895). The next day had a better start: "Last scene, a fine piece of painting, better than London" but then Hochberg told him "that the opera must be postponed a week" because "neither primadonna could be present". Due to these developments and sickness, the composer must have been in an extremely bad mood when he wrote to Wilfred Bendall on 16 November 1895: "Bad luck still pursues *Ivanhoe* here. [Note in the margin: Two nice active heroines – Rebecca a sprained knee and Rowena acute lumbago!] I am not sanguine about the success at all . . . None of them except King Richard have two-pennyworth of voice, nor can they sing. The chorus is awful . . . They all tell me they have spent 70,000 marks [£3,500] on the production but I told Pierson [the administrative director] today, I don't see more than 20,000 at present. The most satisfactory part is the orchestra and the excellent little conductor, Dr. Muck."[70] Sullivan seems to have been on the verge of leaving before the first night but "Hochberg insisted upon my stay for it, said it made all the difference between success and failure. So I gave way."

Indeed, Sullivan was not always satisfied with what he saw at rehearsals. "Scene changing very slow . . . disappointed in dresses – very dowdy and lacking entirely in brilliancy. No Rebecca and Rowena yet. Hochberg decided to postpone till 26th (16 November 1895). The next day Sullivan visited Hiedler, who had had an accident – "She can hardly walk. . ." – so it is not surprising that he "felt wretchedly ill and depressed in the morning. Stayed in bed till 1:30". On the 23rd November the composer finally saw a "good long rehearsal" and noted a "call for Bertie" (his nephew) and "Auntie left Paris" (Ms. Fanny Ronalds). No wonder that after a nerve-racking time, with the weather still "bitterly cold", he "went to circus Renz" two days before the first night in order to find some diversion.

The "full dress rehearsal" (Generalprobe) took place on 25 November at 11:30 a.m. "Emperor expected but did not come", Sullivan recalled in his diary and came to the following conclusion: "All went like clockwork. It won't be a very great success, but it won't be a failure." In the afternoon the Berlin photograph of Sullivan was taken at J.C. Schaarwachter which was also distributed as a postcard.[71] The local press showed great interest before the performance and *Ivanhoe* got some noticeable pre-publicity, for example with a long interview in the *Berliner Tageblatt* of 25 November. Expectations were high but there were also people waiting for an opportunity to destroy Sullivan's fondest dreams.

The first night and its aftermath

The importance of the Berlin première and Sullivan's confidence is revealed in the meticulous handwriting in the diary of late November 1895. He experienced the decisive day as follows: "Strolled out a little in the afternoon with Bertie. Dined in my room at ¼ to 7. Then to theatre. House crowded. Emperor and Empress arrived soon after 7:30. Then the opera began. First act seemed dull. The tournament ought to come out – it is 'kindisch'.[72] I think 2nd act worked splendidly. Hiedler and Bulss very fine. I got an enthusiastic call at the end. 3rd act went well but Wiener (?) couldn't quite make it out, too much melodrama. 4th act splendid, & I got another enthusiastic call. Then I was sent for by the Emperor, who chatted a long time with me and the Empress. His M. was *most* enthusiastic and said 'this opera I must come and see many times. It is beautiful.' (I hope he will have the chance given him. Bertie and I supped at Wiener Café. Then home – sleepless. Many callers in the morning. Left at 1:10 arr. Cologne 11 p.m. Slept Hotel du Nord. Wrote to Hochberg, Brandt."

A look at the reviews gives the impression that Sullivan had spent that night in another theatre. "What you can hear withdraws in the background and accordingly the reception was half-hearted", the reviewer of the *Vossische Zeitung* reported. "There was an icy coolness after the first act; the hands did not move. After the second and the last act there was mild applause which called the composer who was present on the stage . . ."[73] Sullivan's impression on the day before the première that "it won't be a very great success, but it won't be a failure . . ." seemed to be a misjudgement. In the following weeks the opera house fulfilled its duty with ten (instead of the scheduled twelve) performances during the 1895/96 season,[74] which was and still is a good and normal average. In spite of that, *Ivanhoe* has never returned to the Berlin or any other professional stage and the work failed to enter the repertoire. What had happened?

In the late 19th century the Berlin *Ivanhoe* was a failure – as had been destiny of the *Goldene Legende* in Berlin eight years before – despite some positive reactions. This was by no means the fault of the productions or the artists involved. There was particular praise for "especially Ms Goetze, Mr Krolop and Bulss were excellent" (*Berliner Tageblatt*, 27 November 1895) whereas for others "Kapellmeister Muck and the gentlemen Sylva and Bulss as well as the ladies Weitz and Hiedler were best" (*Vossische Zeitung*, 27 November 1895). In the *Neue Zeitschrift für Musik* (1 January 1896) we even get some description of the looks and the acting: "Miss Hiedler was a touching Rebecca in her singing and acting . . .; Mr Bulss a satanic seducer . . .; Ms Goetze was remarkable in the small role as Ulrica, the voice suited excellently to the sad oriental tunes and her charming appearance revealed itself despite the flattering white hair, the hollow eyes and the deathlike pallor; but it turned the weird Ulrica into a more desirable person than intended by the authors. . ." The music magazine continued that "Kapellmeister Muck conducted with admirable 'maestra' and certainty helped even the weaker numbers of the opera to a relatively positive effect".[75]

Technically the production was a masterly achievement. The influential *Berliner Tageblatt* was enthusiastic: "You cannot imagine anything more spectacular than the production of this opera. These sets alone are worth seeing . . ."[76] For others it "surpasses anything that you have ever seen at the Royal Opera House" (*Vossische Zeitung*, 27 November 1895). The production team did everything they could that "the scenic devices worked exemplarily; they present unusual demands for the producer and the stage mechanic with its repeated change of decoration with the open curtain and its mass groupings" (*Signale für die musikalische Welt*, 29 November 1895).

Although the building of the Staatsoper Unter den Linden today is basically the former opera house of the Königliche Schauspiele, sometimes called "Hofoper", the technical devices of those days were totally different. In the late 19th century the Hofoper did not have side

SIR WALTER SCOTT
1771 - 1832

stages (which were not added until the reconstruction in 1926-28) nor a stage tower (for lowering the sets). Even the acoustics cannot be compared to the former building since the old opera house had four balconies up to World War II (for about 1,800 people altogether) whereas today there are only three balconies for safety reasons and a better view (for 1,452 people). The size of the stage remained: It is 13 metres wide and 7.50 metres high with a total of about 1,200 square metres. The pit had the capacity for a big and strong orchestra.[77]

According to the reports, *Ivanhoe* featured "right and disguised princes, templars, monks, jews and jewesses, lots of horses" as well as castles, chambers, fields, gardens, woods and "the burning of the castle in Torquilstone must be called a fantastic achievement of theatre decoration and machinery".[78] However the dramatic fluency of the action that, as mentioned above, is reminiscent of the video-clip technique used these days, was too much of a good thing for one reviewer who complained that "the libretto presents a muddled-up confusion . . . . chaos of situation, events, changes, and strange people so that it would be difficult to describe the action approximately . . . I followed the plot on stage closely, but the connections are not clear yet. When you think that you have got a clue --- bang! the scenery changes; and when after a while you hope that you have grasped the saving thread of the story, it won't last long because in the next moment everything vanishes and changes into something completely different. So we see right and disguised princes, templars, monks, jews and jewesses; lots of horses, castles, chambers, fields, gardens and forests coming and clearing out that you feel dizzy."[79]

Without our common electrical devices or computerised scene changes, the workers had to rely on painted backcloth and light for suggesting the different atmospheres. Despite these drawbacks, some scene changes probably did not take too long because there were various opportunities to use the depth of the stage with some more intimate scenes closer to the pit or the whole stage for mass scenes.

Ivanhoe's last stand

Unfortunately, the general attitude towards the Berlin performance was that the eyes were much more pleased than the ears as the scenery was "much more brilliant than the new piece, wasted for a weak opus but it will assure some more performances" (*Musikalisches Wochenblatt*, 5 December 1895). In general, reviews at that time were somewhat different from today. There was hardly anything about the "message" of the production and certainly nothing about the concept of the production team. Since a lot of the operas in the repertoire were new works, reviewers mainly focused on describing and assessing the pieces. In many cases there was just general praise of the artists with hardly any detailed descriptions of voices or individual interpretations.

Concerning Sullivan's *Ivanhoe* version itself, almost all of the reviewers had a negative attitude which sometimes led to even hostile reviews. Some of the milder versions stated that the "new opera received a mild rejection which was justified as the new work has a musical meagreness without parallel" (*Musikalisches Wochenblatt*, 5th December 1895) or that "Sullivan's music is not outstanding but parts of it are very pleasing, especially in the lyrical and humorous numbers of the score. The composer achieves a dramatic effect only in the last act which, after the second, can be called the best one . . . The opera did not take sympathy of the audience by storm . . . Not until the second act the applause became stronger and increased until the end so that after all we can call it a good success. Sullivan, who was present at the first night, was called several times" (*Signale für die musikalische Welt*, 29 November 1895). The latter was confirmed by Sullivan's diaries.

These assessments, however, remained exceptions among the mainly slating reviews:

> Based on Walter Scott's novel they threw a libretto together with the most worn-out, the most remote stereotyped methods of old opera. Concerning incomprehensibleness and incoherence it can rival with the worst models. And for this lousy miserable concoction the ingenious composer of *The Mikado* wrote music that is so meaningless and dull in its invention, so conventional in its making, so void of individuality that it equals the libretto accordingly. A great deal of industry, a great deal of care and attention and – above all – a great deal of money was wasted on this performance. The opera could not be saved despite the splendid sets. (*Allgemeine Musik-Zeitung*, 6 December 1895)

> A funeral . . ., the cool, icy reception meant nothing but 'requiescat in pace!' . . . Is it justified? We have to say 'yes'. . . . libretto: a chaotic mess . . . When it comes to the music a strange mixture of a light operetta and oratorio style becomes apparent. The latter one proves that the composer had cultivated serious studies, too, but in spite of that the lighter numbers show that his talent lies with the first one. Alas, only for the grand dramatic opera the powers of the English maestro do not seem to be sufficient. When there are opportunities of dramatic situations such as the rape of the jewess by the templar or when Rebecca, accused of witchcraft, should be burnt on the stake while the templar wants to save her, the author did not make use of them and wrote completely unimportant music." (*Neue Zeitschrift für Musik*, 1 January 1896)

The critic of the *Neue Zeitschrift für Musik* picks out some musical numbers and describes Cedric's drinking song as "an oratorio number". For him Rowena's aria with harp accompaniment is similar to Wagner's "Winterstürme wichen dem Wonnemond" and although the Rowena – Ivanhoe duet has "some dramatic accents", the following song by King Richard is "weak and it caused some ironic laughing when Friar Tuck exclaimed his optimistic words "kein schlechtes Lied" (not a bad song). Friar Tuck's song was "an operetta-like chansonette" but "effective" – according to the reviewer it gives "a hint in which direction Sullivan should follow his muse . . .". Some attraction was caused, at least by characteristic "oriental songs" in the same act, while in the third act there was a strange slumber song which Ivanhoe sings to himself when he tries to fall asleep, not to speak of the last act which was "musically even weaker" with "nothing worth mentioning". As if some of the critics had chatted during the interval, there were comparisons between Sullivan and Johann Strauss: "Sullivan also wanted to write a grand opera. This brings more honour to his artistic ambition than to his ability of self-assessment . . . *Ivanhoe*, which is dear to his heart as all the children who turned out badly are to their fathers, has proved to be completely ineffective . . ." (*Berliner Tageblatt*, 27 November 1895). "It won't live long", was the warning of the *Allgemeine Musik-Zeitung* three days after the première. "Go to see it now . . ." Another reviewer even suggested: "If the public also thinks that 'Ivanhoe' is a failure, it will disappear from the repertoire. The splendid sets may be a reason to revive Marschner's *Templer und die Jüdin*, which has the same topic. That would be no bad exchange." Although the opera house had a new production of Marschner's *Der Vampyr* (16 August 1895), the last production of *Der Templer und die Jüdin* took place in 1830 with no new one to come until or after 1895. The *Ivanhoe* topic was no longer tempting to European audiences.

A new sense of drama

The work itself did not appeal to the critics. Although Nicolai once said: "In Italy the people form their own opinion, in Germany the critics tell them what to think . .", one cannot deny that people vote with their feet, and Sullivan's *Ivanhoe* did not appeal to the majority of the audience either. In his diaries and letters, Sullivan never commented on the Berlin reviews or the rejection of the work in a leading opera house of continental Europe. This may also be seen as a sign of how his confidence transformed into disappointment.

Sullivan lost contact with Count Hochberg until his comic opera *The Mikado* was performed in exactly the same theatre in June 1900. The composer recalled in his diaries: "I spoke to the company and apologized for my ignorance of the opera, not having heard it for many years. Rehearsals till 2:30. Very good on the whole. The principals are all opera artists." The fact that Sullivan stresses the quality of the singers reveals how he would have wanted his works to be performed. A performance of a comic opera was not an exception for the Hofoper because they had works in a similar vein in their regular repertoire.[80]

The failure of *Ivanhoe* in Berlin must also be seen within the context of the regular repertoire, the expectations and the competition of successful new operas of the day. A few months before Sullivan's piece, in May 1895, a new work had its world première in Berlin: *Der Evangelimann* (*The Evangelist*) by Wilhelm Kienzl (1857–1941). It had the same male leads but a totally different sense of drama due to a *verismo* influence, sweetened by wonderful lyrical orchestral passages. The topic did not lead back to the crusades but referred to the modern days. In addition, it was based on a true story.[81] Certainly people would have expected something like the dramatic impact of the confrontation between Martha and Johannes in act 1 in the duet of the Templar and Rebecca. Apart from modern topics of the day with stories that were true to life and believable (such as *Der Evangelimann*, *Cavalleria rusticana* etc.), the repertoire that "surrounded" the *Ivanhoe* performances[82] was mainly focused on Wagner. Although one might say: "That's historic, too . . .", the major difference is that Scott/Sturgis/Sullivan *invented* characters in a historic surrounding whereas Wagner's "history" is safely *rooted* in Germanic and Nordic legends that became archetypes for the Germans. Wagner's plots were therefore much closer to the sense and sensibility of the people (as was the pathetic music).

Other problems for *Ivanhoe* may include a negative attitude towards foreign operas (which were probably performed due to an order by the Kaiser). There was a general artistic and political climate that made it difficult for foreigners. Even in reviews, that were suppose to be written by educated, open-minded people, there were sometimes statements such as: "In the 10 concerts of the Gewandhaus orchestra they made a huge issue of this foreigner business . . ." ("Im 10. Gewandhauskonzert ... hat die *Ausländerei* eine große Rolle gespielt . . .", in *Signale für die musikalische Welt*, No 67, Leipzig, 20 December 1895). The hint, mentioned above, to revive Marschner's opera, reveals a tendency of that time towards "generally go to German operas". Certainly, because a lot of Germans thought that for peoples such as the English music is connected strongly to making money. In a short report about Sullivan's *The Absent-minded Beggar* and *Rose of Persia* the *Neue Zeitschrift für Musik* remarks, "when it comes to making gold out of music the English are almost unique . . ."[83]

Another problem for Sullivan on the continent was that by the mid-1890s the great success of *The Mikado* suppressed an unbiased view of his output.[84] Although *The Mikado* and other of his comic works could be seen in – as Sullivan wrote - "weak performance(s)" the focus on his comic output remained. It was a difficult time for his idea of a compromise between the three main schools of opera. With his concept of "a selection of the merits of each one", Sullivan swam against the tide which praised the tendency to development and progress in music. Sullivan's opera arrived at a time when the idea of evolution crept into the assessment of music history.[85] Nobody noticed the aspect that in his dramatic works (*The Martyr of Antioch*, *The Golden Legend*, *Ivanhoe* etc.) Sullivan adopts a more homogeneous style, whereas in comic operas he makes use of the method Mozart adopted for *The Magic Flute* with a mixture of various styles. There is a different "cloth" for each piece of music – Sullivan himself even once used the term that the characters are "clothed with music" by him. In all his works Sullivan treats the characters with empathy and respect. Sullivan's style may be described as "classical pluralism". "Classical" in the transparent handling of the orchestra (even with large forces)[86]; "pluralistic" in the way he adopts any style that he thinks is adequate for the characterisation of atmosphere, scene or person. Eventually this is a very democratic approach.[87] Did people take notice of his intentions?

According to the diaries, Sullivan was "sleepless" on the night of the Berlin première. This production did matter to him although an even bigger disappointment might have been the Leeds affair of 1898.[88] Both incidents were not mentioned in Arthur Lawrence's biography of 1899. (It is actually no surprise that they were not mentioned in the diaries where Sullivan's biggest emotional outburst occurred when his dog died on 31 December 1890, about a month before the world première of *Ivanhoe*.)

Nevertheless Sullivan seems to have been full of ideas with contacts to the above mentioned Axel Delmar and – as the *Neue Berliner Musikzeitung* mentions on 28 November 1895 – plans for the forthcoming opera *Olivia* with a libretto by Sir Augustus Harris based on Oliver Goldsmith's novel *The Vicar of Wakefield*. Probably he was too ill to realise all his plans. There were complaints about health problems in Berlin, too, which contributed to his declining powers. He was probably no longer able to write another romantic opera on a big scale. The final nail in *Ivanhoe*'s coffin came in the German obituaries in 1900. If it is mentioned at all, it plays a minor part because "his world-wide reputation is based on his opera burlesque 'Der Mikado' which in invention and form towers high above his foreign colleagues in this field from the artistic point of view . . . Sullivan had full control of the trade of his art and possessed a strong and strange talent for musical humour and easily flowing melody . . . His serious opera 'Ivanhoe' turned out to be a very weak work."[89] Interestingly enough, there was also a declining interest in his competitor Wilhelm Kienzl, who suffered similar disappointments. Concerning his failure with *Don Quichotte* he remarked about German audiences: "I should have borne in mind that the public in general does not concern itself with problems but only wants to be gripped in some way or other, that it wants to and can only laugh or only cry."[90]

The right opera at the wrong time?

To sum up the analysis of other *Ivanhoe* operas and the fate of the 1895/96 Berlin production we can come to the conclusion that Sullivan's opera is by far the best *Ivanhoe* version of the 19th century due to its cohesion and its faithfulness to the original source. Were the Berlin reactions justified or is it a work that can find its place in the opera repertoire?

Although it was the first opera that did justice to Scott, it probably arrived at the wrong time. Had it been written twenty years earlier it would have created a sensation; in the 1890s it was superseded by new developments in opera. The crucial aspect remains: Can and should we stage *Ivanhoe* today? If "yes", we need to find answers to the following question: What does the plot, the music and the emotions mean to us, to modern listeners of today? The fact that there is lots of wonderful music is not enough, if we cannot answer these aspects in a convincing way, a performance will definitely fail.

Some suggestions from the continental perspective might help to put the discussion on a more general level: The background of English history was not especially interesting for a German audience of the 1890s, but today it could be emphasised that the opera shows a multicultural society which is an important topic for European audiences as well.

In *Ivanhoe* Sullivan carries forth the approach of Verdi, Meyerbeer and Marschner etc. of opera as mass entertainment. There are great demands for singing-actors and scenery that can be used to create impressive effects (even on an empty stage with thrilling light design). The background of an anti-élite mentality might apply to a large variety of visitors.

It is a "romantic" opera with a strange dramatic finale (sudden death of the villain) but that is true to the novel. In general *Ivanhoe* is a very optimistic opera – with parallels to *Simone Boccanegra* of 1881 (ten years earlier) with its grand *pace* (peace)-ensemble. Both works foster a political utopia. Sullivan's utopia was probably that courage and heart will overcome all difficulties which was certainly in contrast to the general *fin-de-siècle* mood. So *Ivanhoe* remains a forward-thinking opera which is in favour of multi-cultural society – and reveals a similar "massive hope in the future" like Elgar's first symphony later. The opera shows the fight for freedom and justice – one should help the others regardless of religion or origin. It is also pro-Jewish with Rebecca's aria as *the* antithesis to Wagner! No wonder, that in the field of opera there was no chance for *Ivanhoe* in the xenophobic, imperialistic mood of the late 19th century and early 20th century in England and Germany.

Can the work still be appreciated after the world wars with the clothing and sets of the *Ivanhoe* film of 1952 in mind? Probably after 1945 we have a better understanding of people who are not keen on being heroes if fighting is not really necessary. Ivanhoe is a weak, passive and – in this respect – almost a modern protagonist or even anti-hero.[91] It is a realistic portrait of a man who is no hero from top to toe, but who gathers strength when needed and fights against injustice when necessary. Sullivan's work is an opera with sensitive portraits of characters: not only Ivanhoe's or the ladies' but even of the human side of villains as in the templar's big monologue.

The arrangement of the story is closer to the dramaturgy of slavic opera where a "linear" story, as in western dramaturgy, is hardly known (as in *Boris Godunow*, *Chovantchina* or *Evgenij Onegin*). Here the work is split up in several episodes full of impressions and mood with longer time spans between the acts. Nevertheless, the problem is not so much the music, but the story and its background: If an *Ivanhoe* production raises memories of the 1950s Hollywood film, it will fail on stage. Only an opera that works in abstract scenery with good singing actors can be revived and can survive. That's the current continental point of view:

All *Ivanhoe* operas dropped out of the repertoire because at a certain time (late 19th century or early 20th century) people could no longer answer the question: What does it mean to us *today*? Of course, Sullivan's *Ivanhoe* went out of the repertoire too early and for a long time but it should be taken into consideration that under Carte's management and his policy, it hardly had the chance of becoming a pillar in a repertoire of English opera.

Today we have a new chance of re-thinking and approaching the work objectively. The German translator of the *Ivanhoe* libretto, Hugo Wittmann, once wrote: "Art belongs to the eternal things which infuse life into this dead world."[92] One failure does not mean that Sullivan's *Ivanhoe* is not able to inspire our world in future.

IL
TEMPLARIO

MELODRAMMA IN TRE ATTI

DA RAPPRESENTARSI

NEL TEATRO DELLA SOCIETA

Il Carnovale 1841-42.

BERGAMO
DALLA STAMPERIA CRESCINI
1841.

Das Aufführungsrecht ist ausschließlich durch B. Bernstein
in Berlin zu beziehen.

Ivanhoe.

Romantische Oper in 4 Acten nach Walter Scotts
gleichnamigem Roman
von
Julian Sturgis.

Musik von Arthur Sullivan.

für die deutsche Bühne bearbeit von H. Wittmann.

Alle Rechte mit Hinweis auf § 50 des Gesetzes vom
11. Juni 1870 vorbehalten.

Den Bühnen gegenüber als Manuskript gedruckt.

 Text-Buch.

Berlin.
Verlag von P. Bernstein.

TABLE 1

IVANHOE – STRUCTURE OF THE OPERAS

ROSSINI 1826	MARSCHNER 1829	NICOLAI 1840	SULLIVAN 1891	SCOTT/SULLIVAN
(1) Hall of Rotherwood	(I/1) A wild romantic glen: De Bracy, Bois Guilbert		(I/1) Hall of Rotherwood	Chapter 3, 4, 5, 15
			(I/2) Ante-Chamber in Rotherwood	Chapter 6
		(I/1) Lists at Ashby (I/2) Rotherwood	(I/3) Lists at Ashby	Chapter 12, 16, 7
	(I/2) Friar Tuck's hut in the forest (I/3) De Bracy's Castle		(II/1) The Forest (Friar Tuck's hut) (II/2) A Passageway in Torquilstone	Chapter 16, 17, 32 Chapter 23
(II) Castle of St Edmond: Leila. Bois Guilbert	(I/4) A Courtyard inside the Castle: Rebecca, BoisGuilbert	(II/1) A Turret Chamber in Torquilstone	(II/3) A Turret Chamber in Torquilstone	Chapter 31, 24
	(I/5) Courtyard: Burning of the Castle		(II/1) A room in Torquilstone; Assault; Burning of the Castle	Chapter 28. 29, 31, 40
	(II/1) A forest clearing: Richard and the outlaws			
	(II/2) Hall of Justice at Templestowe	(II/2) Templestowe		
	(II/3) The Tournament grounds			
		(II/3) Rotherwood: Reconciliation	(III/2) The Forest: Pardoning of De Bracy	Chapter 32, 42
	(III/2) A Dungeon at Templestowe			
(III) Outside the Castle of St Edmond	(III/3) The Tournament Grounds	(III) Templestowe	(III/3) Percepotory of the Templars at Templestowe	Chapter 37, 43, 44

TABLE II

GIOACCHINO ROSSINI / ANTONIO PACINI: IVANHOÉ (1826)

SCENE	NUMBER	DEFINITION	REFERENCE	STYLE
ACT 1		*Overture*	*Semiramide*	Melodramma tragico
1	1	Introduction and Chorus	*Cenerentola:* Act 2 Scene 6	Drama giocoso
2		Trio and Chorus	Act 1 Scene 4	
3		Stretta, Quartet	Act 1 Scene 6	
2	2	Aria: Ismael and Chorus	*Cenerentola:* Aria of Don Magnifico	
4	3	Aria: Ivanoé	*Bianca e Faliero:* Aria of Contareno Act 1 Scene 8	melodramma
5		Horn solo	London Autograph	
6-7	4	Quartet and Chorus	*Armida:* Act 1 Scene 3	dramma
		Intercalated Recit	London Autograph	
8	5	Chorus	*Maometto II:* Act 2 Scene 6	dramma
9	6	Finale: Duet and Chorus	*Aureliano in Palmira:* Act 1 Scenes 2-3	Drama serio
10		Quartet and Chorus	*La gazza ladra* Act 2 Scene 11	melodramma
		Stretta	*Armida:* Act 1 Scene 13 finale	
ACT 2				
1	7	Aria: Leila	*Sigismundo:* Aria of Sigismundo Act 2 Scene 16	dramma
2	8	Duet	*Torvaldo e Dorlinska* Act 1 Scene 5	Drama semiserio
5-6	9	Trio	*Mosè:* Act 3 Scene 3	Azione tragico-sacra
8	10	Finale: Chorus	*La gazza ladra:* Act 2 Scene 9	
		Judgement trio and Chorus	*Semiramide:* Act 1 Scene 8	
		Quartet and Chorus	*Mosè:* Act 1 Scene 7	
	11	Entr'acte Instrumental	*Semiramide:* Act 1 Scene 2	
ACT 3				
2	12	Chorus	*Tancredi:* Act 3 Scene 16	Melodrama eroico
7	13	Scene and Aria: Boisguilbert	*Semiramide:* Act 2 Scene 9	
8		Boisguilbert & Chorus		
9	14	March and Chorus	*Bianca e Faliero:* Act 2 Scene 7	
		Fanfare	*Passo dopio* for military band, 1822 (?)	
12	15	Finale	*Torvaldo e Dorliska:* Act 1 Scenes 10-11 finale	

TABLE III

MARSCHNER: DER TEMPLER UND DIE JÜDIN (1829/30)

OVERTURE

ACT 1

SCENE 1: A wild romantic glen in the forest

No 1: Introduction (Bracy, Guilbert, Chorus) "Ihr lagert still euch dort im Wald"

Dialogue: Cedric-Oswald etc. or Recitative Rowena "Schon glänzt das Abendrot"

No 2: Song (Wamba) "'s wird besser geh'n"

Dialogue: Cedric-Wamba

Dialogue: Oswald-Cedric or Recitative Oswald "Verweilet länger nicht"

No 3: (Battle song of the Saxons) "Wer Kraft und Mut"

SCENE 2: Inside Friar Tuck's hut in the forest

Dialogue: Black Knight-Tuck

No 4: (Song with Chorus) (Friar Tuck) "Der Barfüsser Mönch"

Dialogue: Locksly-Tuck-Black-Knight

[De Bracy's castle: dialogue & song No 2 & dialogue & 4a trio Cedric-Bracy-Rowena]

SCENE 3: An apartment in a castle turret

No 5: Recitativ (Rebecca) "Wie bang ist mir!"

Dialogue: Guilbert-Rebecca

No 6: (Grand scene & duet with chorus) (Guilbert, Rebecca) "Erkenne mich"

Dialogue: Ivanhoe-Rebecca

No 7: Duet (Rebecca, Ivanhoe) "Teures Mädchen, sagt er – wem?"

No 8: Finale "Horch! Welcher Lärm! Ich höre Waffenklang!"

ACT 2

SCENE 1: A forest clearing

No 9: Introduction (Chorus of Yeomen & Saxons) "Es zittert im Frührot"

Dialogue: Black Knight-Tuck

No 10: Song with chorus (Friar Tuck) "Brüder wacht! Habet acht!"

No 11: Aria with chorus (Ivanhoe) "Es ist dem König Ehr' und Ruhm"

SCENE 2: The hall of justice at Templestowe

Dialogue: Malvoisin-Guilbert

No 12: Scene and aria (Guilbert) "!Mich zu verschmähen!"

SCENE 3: The tournament grounds

No 13: Finale "Wie so ernst und feierlich"

ACT 3

SCENE 1: Grand vestibule of Cedric's castle

No 14: Introduction (Chorus and romance) "Schlinget frohe Tänze"

Dialogue: Wamba

No 15: Song (Wamba) "Es ist doch gar köstlich"

Dialogue: Wamba-Isaak-Ivanhoe

SCENE 2: A dungeon in Templestowe

No 16: Preghiera (Rebecca) "Herr, aus tiefen Jammersnöten"

No 17: Scene and duet (Rebecca, Guilbert) "Wer klopft?"

SCENE 3: The tournament grounds

No 18: Finale "Hier steht der tapf're Ritter"

96

TABLE IV

NICOLAI – IL TEMPLARIO (1840)

Sinfonia (Overture)

ACT1

SCENE 1 (Grand salon at Ashby)

No 1: Ensemble & Chorus "Delle trombe il suon guerriero"

SCENE 2 (Vilfredo d'Ivanhoe enters)

No 2: Cavatina "Sia meco avverso il fato"

SCENE 3 (Camp of Briano de Bois-Guilbert & the Normans)

No 3: Briano's recitative & cavatina "Delle oriantal la traccia"

SCENE 4 (Grand vestibule of Cedrico's castle)

No 4: Chorus of ladies & Rovena's aria "Del cielo britanno... Oh bel sogno lusinghier"

SCENE 5 (Rebecca & Isacco enter)

No 5: Trio & Rebecca's cavatina "Aita! Aita! Ah, salvaci!" & "Ah, quel guardo non celar"

SCENE 6 (The Normans enter)

No 6: Briano & chorus "Si celi ognun"

SCENE 7 (Cedrico approaches the Normans)

No 7: "Quale cagion invia, te, normanno?"

SCENE 8 (The ladies appear; Rovena holds Rebecca's hand)

No 8: Scene "Te Rebecca il cavaliero qual sua schiava a noi richiede" & Sextet "Chiuso nel sen di fremere."

SCENE 9: Finale

No 9: Ensemble "Padre! Oh ciel!"

ACT 2

SCENE 1 (Within the walls of the Templars' castle)

No 10: Rebecca's aria "Vilfredo! Oh nome! Oh rimembranza!"

Scene 2 (Briano enters)

No 11: Duet "O cielo! ... Non fuggir!"

SCENE 3 (Gran sala d'armi nella Commendata)

No 12: March & chorus of the Templars "Morte a leon vorace!"

No 13: Scene Isaaco and ensemble "Pietà! Pietà, signo!"

SCENE 4 (Room of Cedrico's castle)

No14: Duet (Vilfredo-Cedrico) "Desso mio figlio!"

No 15: Trio Vilfredo-Cedrico-Rovena "A suoi prieghi unisco i miei!"

ACT 3

SCENE 1 (Outside the Templars' castle)

No 16: Templars' chorus "Morte a leon vorace ... La dannata è a voi d'innante!"

SCENE 2 (Vilfredo and others enter)

No 17: ensemble "Dell'infelice il difensor son io!"

SCENE 3 (Rebecca, Isaacco & women on stage, combat out of sight)

No 18: ensemble "Quai grida! Chi vinse?"

SCENA ULTIMA (Everyone re-enters)

No 19: ensemble "Signor. . . a tuoi piedi ..."

TABLE V

IVANHOE – ORCHESTRA

	ROSSINI 1826 1 hr 45 min	MARSCHNER 1829 3 hrs 15 min	NICOLAI 1840 2 hrs 30 min	SULLIVAN 1891 3 hrs
ORCHESTRA WOODWIND				
PICCOLO	-	1	1	1
FLUTE	2	2	2	2
OBOE	2	2	2	2
CLARINET	2	2	2	2
BASSOON	2	2	2	2
COR ANGLAIS	-	-	1	1
BASS CLARINET	-	-	-	1
BRASS				
HORN	4	4	4	4
TRUMPET	2	2	2	2
TROMBONE	3	3	3	3
OPHICLEIDE	-	-	1	-
BASS TUBA	-	-	-	1
KETTLEDRUM	-	1	1	-
PERCUSSION INSTRUMENTS	Timpani	-	Bass & side drum, cymbals Tam-tam, triangle	Timpani, bass drum, cymbals
HARP	-	1	1	1
MUSIC ON STAGE	-	Picc, Fl, Ob, 2 clar, 2 bs, 6Hr, 2tr, 2 tro, bass tuba, tambourine	Banda	Bass trumpets

NOTES

1) Eckermann, Johann Peter: *Gespräche mit Goethe in den letzten Jahren seines Lebens*, volume 3, published 1836-48).

2) Heine, Heinrich: *Reisebilder: Englische Fragmente, IV. Teil*, Frankfurt 1980, p. 520; first edition: 1826.

3) In the author's collection there is a *Kenilworth* edition of 1941 and an *Ivanhoe* edition with no date, but without any doubt it is an edition of the first half of the 20th century.

4) Müllenbrock, Hans-Joachim: *Scott und der historische Roman*, in *Die Neueren Sprachen*, November 1972, p. 661 ff.

5) Müllenbrock, Hans-Joachim: *Scott und der historische Roman*, in *Die Neueren Sprachen*, November 1972, p. 663.

6) Even nowadays there is still an enormous interest in historic novels due to an increasing interest in things historic. A writer of historic novels told me that today publishers preferred writers who had studied history. A novel can reach a wider audience and is the more exciting form of presenting complex historic events.

7) There is even a book on operas based on works by Scott: Mitchell, Jerome: The Walter Scott Operas, The University of Alabama Press 1977.

8) For details see: See: Saremba, M.: *In the Purgatory of Tradition – Arthur Sullivan and the English Musical Renaissance*, in In Brüstle, Christa / Heldt, Guido: *Music as a Bridge – Musikalische Beziehungen zwischen England und Deutschland*, Olms Verlag, Hildesheim/New York 2005, p. 33 – 71.

9) Jacobs, Arthur: *Arthur Sullivan – A Victorian Musician*, Aldershot 1992 (second edition), p. 223.

10) Leipzig may have been on his mind around the time of the interview. On the same day we find in his diary – hardly legible, with pencil instead of ink: "Leipzig 1876".

11) Kruse: Nicolai – *Musikalische Aufsätze*, Regensburg 1913, p. 78.

12) Nicolai's operas included: *Rosmonda d'Inghilterra* (Triest 1839 as *Enrico II*), *Il Templario* (Torino 1840), *Gildippe ed Odoardo* (Genova 1840), *Il Proscritto* (Milan 1841; new version as *Die Heimkehr des Verbannten* in Vienna 1844), *Die lustigen Weiber von Windsor* (Berlin 1849).

13) As an admirer of Schumann it is thoroughly possible that Sullivan read older editions of his magazine. Schumann criticised Nicolai's ideas and it is highly probably that Leipzig students discussed operatic aesthetics with their teachers. Sullivan had learned German before he went to Leipzig and spoke the language fluently with hardly any accent until the end of his life as letters and reports in German newspapers reveal (*Berliner Tageblatt*, Abend-Ausgabe, 25th November 1895, p. 1 f.).

14) In interviews and the biography by Arthur Lawrence (1899) Sullivan stated: "I think that he first inspired me with a love for the stage and things operatic. Up to the time from his death I continued to visit Rossini every time I went over to Paris, and nothing occurred to interfere with the cordiality of our friendship." When they chatted it is not unrealistic that Rossini mentioned his operas based on British writers such as *Lucia di Lammermoor* (Scott's *The Bride of Lammermoor*), *La Donna del Lago* (*The Lady of the Lake*) and *Ivanhoé* arranged for Paris.

15) Marschner's operas included: *Heinrich IV und d'Aubigné* (1820), Der Vampyr (1828), *Der Templer und die Jüdin* (1829), *Des Falkners Braut* (1832), *Hans Heiling* (1833), *Das Schloss am Ätna* (1836), *Der Bäbu* (1838), *Kaiser Adolph von Nassau* (1845), *Austin* (1852), *Sangeskönig Hiarne* (1863).

16) Concerning information on all the others of the ten *Ivanhoe* operas see Mitchell, Jerome: *The Walter Scott Operas*, The University of Alabama Press, 1977.

17) Other examples included: Rossini's *Robert Bruce* (with Louis Niedermeyer, Swiss composer; 1846 for Paris Opéra, based on *La Donna del Lago* and other Rossini operas; based on Scott's *Tales of a Grandfather*).

18) The new Théatre de l'Odéon had opened in 1824. The repertoire already included Rossini's *Barbiere di Siviglia, La Gazza Ladra, Otello* and *La Donna del Lago* as opéra comique in French (which are operas with dialogue, not comic operas which are called "opéra bouffe"). The Odéon management commissioned Rossini to write a pastiche. Rossini was busy with the revision *Maometto II* for L'Opéra for which he needed time to solve some specific problems of declamation etc. This is why he worked together with Antonio Pacini.

19) Scott on 31st October 1826; quoted in: Mitchell, Jerome: *The Walter Scott Operas*, The University of Alabama Press 1977, p. 8.

20) The fanfares possibly go back to a *Passo doppio* for military band, written in 1822.

21) This practice, known as Parodieverfahren, "parody", was common from Bach to Rossini. Here "parody" is not an ironic imitation but a composer's procedure to take one of the older pieces and turn them into something new. Prominent examples are the well-known overture to *The Barber of Seville* which was taken from the opera *Elisabetta, Regina d'Inghilterra* (where themes reappear in the first act finale) or the reshaping of a complete opera when Rossini turned *Il Viaggio a Reims* into *Le Comte Ory*.

22) Ismael is Isaac of York, Leila is Rebecca, Saint Edmondo is Templestowe, the Templars' castle and headquarters.

23) Concerning a comparison of Sullivan's opera to Walter Scott's novel see Robrahn, Ulrike: "*Ivanhoe* als lyrische Oper (Sullivan) und historischer Roman (Scott) unter Berücksichtigung von werkimmanenter Dramaturgie, öffentlicher Rezeption und Institutionsgeschichte", diploma thesis , Magdeburg 2001, published under the title "Sullivans Ivanhoe – die Oper und ihre literarische Vorlage" on the website "www.sullivan-forschung.de".

24) Mitchell, Jerome: *The Walter Scott Operas*, The University of Alabama Press 1977, p. 146 f.

25) At first Nicolai hated Italian opera when he came to Rome in 1833 (he had accepted post of the organist at the Prussian Embassy). He soon fell in love with Italian music, especially Bellini, and stayed in Rome for 3 years. He travelled to other Italian cities seeking a commission to write an opera (a so-called "scrittura"). He returned to Italy after he was assistant Kapellmeister at the Hoftheater in Vienna in 1837.

26) Nicolai in a letter to his father on 11th February 1840,: "For Italy the orchestra is very good. I sat, as usual, three nights at the harpsichord." ("Das Orchester ist für Italien sehr gut. Ich habe die drei Abende, wie gebräuchlich, am Cembalo gesessen." in Schröder, Berta (ed.): *Otto Nicolais Tagebücher nebst biographischen Ergänzungen*, Leipzig 1892, p. 115.)

27) Mitchell, Jerome: *The Walter Scott Operas*, The University of Alabama Press 1977, p. 156 f.

28) Details in Palmer, A. Dean: *Heinrich August Marschner: His Life and Stage Works*, UMI Research Press, Ann Arbor, Michigan, 1980, p. 102-108.

29) Palmer, A.D.; p. 112-115.

30) Brief vom 11. 12. 1833; vgl. U. Schreiber, A.; Oper, 128 f.

31) Wagner: ". . . mit ihrer vulkanischen, alles durchbrechenden Leidenschaft als eine Schöpfung von größter Eigentümlichkeit der Erfindung und bedeutender, stellenweise sogar genialer melodischer Erfindung." in Wittmann, C.F. (ed.): *Der Templer und die Jüdin*, Leipzig o.J. (about early 20 thcentury), S. 14.

32) Concerning the importance of this aspect in 19th century opera see: Becker, Heinz (ed.): *Die 'Coleur locale' in der Oper des 19. Jahrhunderts*, Regensburg 1976.

33) Devrient wrote in a letter of 14th August 1831: ". . . people found overture too long and not clear enough."

34) The topic of abuse of power, revealed in the Rebecca-Templar complex, is one of the backgrounds of the career of Violetta de Strozzi (1891-1981) who recorded the song in February 1924 with the orchestra of Staatsoper in Berlin, that is the opera house where Sullivan's *Ivanhoe* had its German première. She was born in Sarajewo and from the 1920s onwards a star at the Staatsoper. Since she was married to a Jew, the rise of the Nazis became a major threat to her family. Hermann Göring was especially fond of Violetta de Strozzi. He offered her high sums of money and a leading role in a new opera under the condition that she would abandon her husband and be willing to do some "favours" for the Reichsmarschall. He threatened that her husband would be in danger if she refused – so to some extent Goering became her "Templar". Violetta de Strozzi decided resolutely to emigrate to the USA. By doing so she saved her family but got a nervous breakdown which meant the end of her stage career.

35) The content of the text is similar to Sturgis: "Herr, aus tiefen Jammersnöten hör' der Seele brünstig Flehen, lass mich nicht in Gram vergehen; höre, ach, höre mein Beten! Die mich schmähen, die mich hassen, schreiten groß und stolz einher, zahllos wie der Sand am Meer; ich bin hilflos und verlassen, wenn ich meine Hände ringe, wenn ich weine bitterlich, höhnen meine Feinde mich, niemand, niemand, der mir Trost bringe . . .".

36) Sound elements of jazz, sprirituals or the Broadway are used to create operatic "coleur locale". The title was inspired by Wagner and Debussy (in order to parallel Tristan und Isolde or Pelléas et Melisande). The influence of Italian opera can be found in the love duet "Bess, you is my woman now" (Puccini), whereas the style of the "Buzzard song" reminds of a Mussorgski monologue. There are haunting tunes such as "Summertime" or "I got plenty or 'nuttin'" which, as Gershwin said, Verdi would not have been ashamed of writing. The model for the fugue during the fight and murder in act one resembles the thrashing fugue at the end of the second act of Die Meistersinger von Nürnberg – to mention just a few examples of how Gershwin made use of the virtues of all other styles in order to write his opera of the future. Whether he knew of Sullivan's concept, which was first published in an American newspaper, remains speculation. At least Gershwin visited London where he might have seen the former English National Opera House and works such as Strike Up the Band! and Of Thee I Sing owe a lot to Sullivan's comic operas.

37) *Parsifal* was premièred only ten years earlier. The Berlin reviews mention the demands on the technical staff concerning the fast changes of action in *Ivanhoe*.

38) *Neue Zeitschrift für Musik*, 11th December 1891.

39) When Marschner planned to perform *Der Templer und die Jüdin* in England, the King of England, George IV. (King 1811 – 25th June 1830) had accepted Marschner's dedication of the score to him in 1829/30. Plans for performing the opera were thwarted due to legal bickering between the Adelphi Theatre and the publishing firm (Details in Palmer, A. Dean: *Heinrich August Marschner: His Life and Stage Works*, UMI Research Press, Ann Arbor, Michigan, 1980, p. 100.) The opera was not performed in England until 1840; in 1842 Marschner dedicated his *Grand Overture Solenne*, op. 78 in celebration of the birth of a son to Queen Victoria.

40) Nicolai wrote in a letter to his father on 23rd March 1840): "Tomorrow I am leaving for Genova. The king had ordered marches from me. I was allowed to present them to him personally. The queen accepted the dedication of the opera." ("Nach Genua ... Morgen reise ich dorthin ab. Der König hatte Märsche bei mir bestellt. Ich habe sie ihm persönlich einhändigen dürfen. Die Königin hat die Dedikation der Oper akzeptiert." (Schröder, Berta (ed.): *Otto Nicolais Tagebücher nebst biographischen Ergänzungen*, Leipzig 1892, S. 116.) Since Genoa became part of the Kingdom Sardinia in 1815 (until 1861), the rulers in question must have been Carlo Alberto (king of Sardinia 1831-1849) and his wife Maria Theresia of Tuscany, parents of the well-known Vittorio Emanuele II., the future king of Italy.

41) In a speech of 16th June 1898, on the occasion of the 10th anniversary of his reign, Kaiser Wilhelm II stated that he was rooted in the school of idealism. Due to this fact he wanted that the theatre should become a tool of the monarch as are schools or universities. "Like them, the theatres shall contribute to the education of the spirit and the character and to the refinement of moral attitudes. The theatre is also one of my weapons", the Emperor said and added: "I also thank you for complying with my ideas and requests." The Emperor had an influence on the programme insofar that he claimed, art should raise the people "instead of leading them into the gutter". (see: Quander, Georg (ed.): *Apollini er Musis – 250 Jahre Opernhaus unter den Linden*, Berlin 1992, p. 118.)

42) The Sullivan quotations are taken from the composer's diaries if not otherwise stated. Some books remark that Sullivan did not comment on the Berlin production in his diaries which is by no means true. There are a lot

of entries and – in contrast to his usual procedure – most of them in a very careful handwriting.

43) According to the conductor Ernest Ford the second scene of act two "should have been entirely eliminated... He (Sullivan) once told me that this scene spoilt the act, which, it may be said, with this exception contained the most splendid music of the opera. It is inconceivable that, had he found the opportunity, he would not have composed an entirely new one." This can be doubted since Sullivan had the opportunity between 1893 and 1895 but there not too many cuts in act II/2. The *Daily News* report of 30th September 1892 must also have been a hoax: "Sir Arthur Sullivan has wisely resolved to thoroughly revise his opera 'Ivanhoe', and the production of the work in German at the Imperial Opera House, Berlin, has accordingly been postponed until next year. . . . Certain rumours, which have even found their way into print, to the effect that the composer is taking but scant interest in the Berlin performances are, we have the best reason to believe, quite inaccurate. On the contrary, after he has closed the Leeds Festival, and has enjoyed a very brief holiday, Sir Arthur proposes practically to rewrite the second act of the opera; while throughout the work the tenor hero will have far more greater opportunities, and will be much more in evidence than heretofore. Later, in 1893, *Ivanhoe* in its new and improved form will, we understand, be reintroduced to London." (quotations see Jacobs, Arthur: *Arthur Sullivan*, Aldershot 1992 (second edition), p. 331 and p. 350.)

44) Sullivan went to the second act of *Gondoliers* at the Linden-Theater on 23 November 1893 and judged in his diary: ". . .very bad, tempi all to slow, no "go". . .". When his German agent who looked after Sullivan's continental interests, B. Bernstein, called, he told him to ask for injunction against the part of 'Nanki-Poo' being played by a woman, (Ilka von Palmay) in the production of *The Mikado* at the Linden-Theater next Tuesday. A *Mikado* performance at the Friedrich-Wilhelm-Theater on 2 December 1893 was not worth any remarks.

45) Contents of the one-act opera *Mara* (libretto by Axel Delmar; music by Ferdinand Hummel): Caucasia, in our time. The marriage of Eddin and Mara has not softened the conflict between the tribes to which bride and bridegroom belong – it even became worse. In the mountains Eddin gets into a quarrel with his enemies. In order to defend his own life, he shoots at them. Unfortunately the bullet kills the father of his beloved wife. He flees back to his hut where Mara has just sung a lullaby for their son Dmitri. The couple rejoice because of his return but soon Mara learns about the horrible incident that occurred in the mountains. The enemies approach and demand revenge. There remains no time for refuge. Mara's husband hides in a hollow tree. The avengers appear led by Mara's brother Djul. They threaten that little Dmitri will have to pay with his life if they cannot find the culprit. Mara is in despair: Shall she sacrifice her child or her husband? Her love for Eddin wins out. When the avengers want to drag the boy out of the house in order to kill him, Eddin steps out from his hiding-place to take on the challenger. They decide not to shoot him, as he had hoped for, but they plan to throw him down the cliff alive where the body of Mara's father was smashed. Mara sees that she cannot save her husband but she does not want him to be tortured. In order to save him from this terrible death, she makes a horrible decision: She shoots the beloved husband herself. Little Dmitri is awake again and Mara carries on playing with the boy as she had done before Eddin arrived.

46) Like the giant gate in RKO's 1933 *King Kong* that was used several times in other films and eventually burned down years later in *Gone With the Wind*.

47) The cuts for the *Ivanhoe* production in the Berlin version of 1895/96 were as follows: (In order to check the cuts easily the timing is based on the 1989 Pearl recording: Sullivan: *Ivanhoe*, The Prince Consort with soloists, chorus and orchestra, conductor: David Lyle; Pearl SHE CDS 9615 (3 CDs)

Act 1, Scenes 1 – 3

Complete.

Act 2, Scene 1 (Outside the Friar's hut)

CD 2 No 2: 0:01 – 0:52 [cut of 0:52] = short passage in dialogue King – Friar

CD 2 No 4: 0:01 – 1:50 [cut of 1:50] = after Tuck's song to "Enter Locksley"

Act 2, Scene 2 (A Passageway in Torquilstone)

CD 2 No 5: 1:12 – 3:24 [cut of 2:12] = passage in dialogue Rowena – De Bracy – Cedric

Act 2, Scene 3 (A Turret Chamber in Torquilstone)

CD 2 No 7: 4:36 – 5:16 [cut of 0:40] = short passage in dialogue Ulrica – Rebecca

CD 2 No 9: 4:57 – 8:53 [cut of 3:55] = part of scene Templar - Rebecca

Act 3, Scene 1 (A Room in Torquilstone)

CD 3 No 3: 0:01 – 2:15 [cut of 2:15] = part of duet Ivanhoe – Rebecca

Act 3, Scene 2 (In the Forest) = Berlin version act 4, scene 1

CD 3 No 4: 1:52 – 7:13 [cut of 5:21] = scene King – Ivanhoe – De Bracy

CD 3 (5) 4:48 – (6) 2:35 [cut of 3:46] = scene King – Ivanhoe – Rowena

Act 3, Scene 3 (The Preceptory of the Templars; Templestowe) = Berlin version act 4, scene 2

CD 3 No 8: 1:12 – 3:34 [cut of 2:22] = scene Grand Master -Rebecca

48) Concerning the attitude of opera audiences in late 19th century Germany see Weiner, Mark: *Richard Wagner and the Anti-Semitic Imagination*, University of Nebraska Press 1995, and Fischer, Jens-Malte: Richard Wagners *Das Judentum in der Musik*, Frankfurt/Leipzig 2000.

49) This can be found in the Geheime Staatsarchiv in Berlin-Dahlem. A lot of the inventory of the archives were destroyed during World War II; it was, for example, not possible to find any sketches for costumes or stage designs of the 1895/96 *Ivanhoe* production.

50) See: Quander, Georg (ed.): *Apollini er Musis – 250 Jahre Opernhaus unter den Linden*, Berlin 1992, p.119.

51) At that time all operas were played in the language of the country – a practice that was common in Germany even on recordings up to the 1960s and 1970s. Today almost all works are performed in the original language, with the exception of comic operas or musicals which are sometimes played in their native language.

52) Like Einstein Mr. Wittmann was born in Ulm on 16 October 1839. He became a journalist, writer and translator. Due to family connections he went to Paris in his youth and lived there for 10 years, but he also travelled through Europe and the USA. In 1872 he moved to Vienna where he lived and worked for half a century until he died on 6th February 1923. Based on his life experience he naturally became francophile and admired Wagner's *Lohgengrin* and *Meistersinger*. Later he was rather critical of the ideology and mysticism of *Parsifal*. Wittmann loved Mozart's da Ponte operas, Haydn and Beethoven. He not only wrote about history, art, theatre and music (among others also essays about Shakespeare translations) but also worked as a librettist with A. Wohlmut for Karl Millöcker (later also Strauss and others).

53) When, for example, in Act I Scene 1 Ivanhoe replies to ". . . second only to our Templar knights!" with his heroic outburst: "Second to *none*!", Wittmann translates: "König Richard's Heer / Sah manchen braven Rittersmann, / Würdig des Ruhmes und der höchsten Ehr', / Und nur uns Tempelrittern nicht voran." Ivanhoe: "Allen *voran*! . . . Allen voran stand Richard's Ritterschaft - Ich melde, was mein Auge sah." Here the sounds of the German words match the English where necessary.

54) The proof how singable Wittmann's translation is, was given on 2 October 2005 in the final concert to the conference of the Sir Arthur Sullivan Society "Sullivanhoe – The Disinherited Opera" when the soprano Katie Leaver agreed at very short notice to sing one verse of Rowena's aria in German. For the first time after 110 years people could hear again these words:

> O Mond, wie Dein Licht dem Silber gleich,
> Erstrahlet in stiller Ruh!
> O Mond ist mein Liebster auch so bleich,
> So bleich wie Du?
> O leuchte auf sein weißes Zelt
> Im fernen, fremden Land,
> Entlocke ihn der feindlichen Welt
> Zurück zum Heimatstrand.

55) Concerning information about the singers see: K.J. Kutsch / Leo Riemens (ed.): *Großes Sängerlexikon, 4. Auflage.*

56) In 1868 Eloi Sylva had made his debut in Nantes, then he went to Brussels and other places. In 1872 Robert le Diable was his first role at Grand Opera in Paris; ten years later he sang Vasco in *L'Africaine* in Berlin. He played Eleazar in *La juive*, the Prophet, Turridu, Canio, Hüon (*Oberon*), Idomeneo Rienzi and Tannhäuser. From 1886 onwards he sang at the Met and was a regular guest in St Petersburg, Moscow and Covent Garden. He also performed in some world premières such as *Genesius* by Felix von Weingarten (15November 1892) or *Der Evangelimann* by Wilhelm Kienzl (4 May 1895). In 1889 he joined the ensemble at the opera of the Königlichen Schauspiele in Berlin up to the end of his career in 1902 (his farewell role in 1902 was Florestan). This may be why he did not leave any recordings. Sylva stayed in Berlin until his death in 1919, but during the First World War he had difficulties since he was a foreigner (he remained a citizen of Belgium).

57) Geheimes Staatsarchiv, Berlin-Dahlem, I. HA, Rep. 89, Nr. 21138 (Geh. Zivilkabinett, jüngere Periode). This and other letters by Count Hochberg to Kaiser Wilhelm II. remained because the management had to ask for permission for all contracts that were higher than 3000 Marks per year. Eloi Sylva had a special contract: from November 1894 to March 1895 and June 1895 he earned: 700 Marks per role (guaranteed 42 performances). From September 1895 onwards he had a five-year contract with 600 Marks per role, guaranteed 60 performances per year. The original says: "Der Engagementvertrag des Sängers Sylva geht mit Ablauf dieser Spielzeit (1893/94) zu Ende. Sylva hat während seiner bisherigen Wirksamkeit an der Königlichen Oper dargethan, daß er ein Heldentenor ersten Ranges ist, der vermöge seiner phänomenalen Stimmmittel, die von erstaunlicher Ausdauer sind, eine feste Stütze für das Repertoir bildet. Bei dem äußerst empfindlichen Mangel an brauchbaren Tenoristen liegt es im dringenden Interesse der Verwaltung, Sylva auf Jahre für die königliche Oper zu gewinnen, da eine ungestörte Durchführung des laufenden Repertoirs ohne ihn nicht denkbar ist." 28.2.1894 (Eingang 8.3., Antwort 12.3.)

58) Paul Bulss was an ensemble member of the opera house of the Königlichen Schauspiele from 1889 to 1901. He died the following year in Temesvar (Timisoara). His debut was in Lübeck in 1868 as the Czar in Lortzing's *Czar and Carpenter*, then he went to Cologne and Kassel. Bulss caused a sensation in concerts at the Gewandhaus in Leipzig as well as at the Dresdener Hofoper between 1876 and 1889. He sang Jago in Verdi's *Otello*, Count Luna, Escamillo, Marschner's Hans Heilig and the Vampyre, Don Giovanni, Count in Mozart's *Figaro* and light operas. He was a regular colleague of Eloi Sylva, for example in Weingarner's operas, Tonio in *Pagliacci* (1892) and Johannes Freudhofer in *Der Evangelimann* (1895).

59) Geheimes Staatsarchiv, Berlin-Dahlem. The original of 2 March 1900 says: " . . .da am 1. September nächsten Jahres der Vertrag mit dem Sänger Bulss endigt, den zu erneuern in meiner Absicht liegt. Jedenfalls müsste der p. Bulss seine Ansprüche sehr bedeutend zurückschrauben."

60) Adrienne Weitz made her debut in Munich in 1887 and at the age of 23 she sang in the première of Wagner's juvelilia *Die Feen*. She came to Berlin in 1888. Her singing career, mainly in lyrical roles, lasted until 1907. She sang roles such as Figaro-countess, Pamina, Zerlina, Euryanthe and Leonora (Beethoven). Later she worked as a teacher.

61) Geheimes Staatsarchiv, Berlin-Dahlem. The original of 19 March 1902 says: "Euerer Kaiserlichen und Königlichen Majestät erlaube ich mir allerunterthänigst zu berichten, daß der Vertrag der seit 1. December 1888 hier engagierten Sängerin Weitz am 30.November vorigen Jahres sein Ende erreichte. Obgleich ich die talentvolle Künstlerin nicht gern missen wollte, ihr aber auch mit Rücksicht auf die beschränkte Verwendbarkeit hinsichtlich ihrer physischen und stimmlichen Kräfte das bisher bezogene Einkommen bestehend in 7500 Mark Gehalt und einem 50 Mal im Jahr garantierten Spielgelde von 50 Mark nicht weiter gewähren konnte, so habe ich mit der genannten Künstlerin einen neuen, am 1. December 1901 beginnenden, bei nicht erfolgter Kündigung von Jahr zu Jahr weiter laufenden 5 jährigen Vertrag vereinbart, der ihr ein Gehalt von 4000 Mark und ein 50 Mal garantirtes Spielgeld von 20 Mark zusichert. Unter diesen Bedingungen bleibt die p. Weitz für das Ensemble der Königlichen Oper immerhin eine schätzenswerte Kraft."

62) Her first role in Berlin was Gounod's Marguerite in 1887. Later she sang Wagner heroines (Elsa, Venus, Elisabeth, Senta, Eva, Freia) and received great reputation as Aida, Pamina, Fidelio-Leonore, Agathe (Meyerbeer) and Herodias in *Salome*. She sang in the world première of Ethel Symth's *Der Wald* (9 April 1902) and performed at Covent Garden in 1907 (Senta). After her farewell performance in 1908 (Sieglinde) she only

sang in concerts. Later she worked as a singing teacher, from 1910 until 1926 she became professor at the Berliner Musikhochschule. There are two rare Columbia recordings of 1904.

63) Geheimes Staatsarchiv, Berlin-Dahlem. The original says: "Die königliche Sängerin Hiedler, welche seit 1887 der Königlichen Oper angehört, hat im Verlauf ihrer künstlerischen Wirksamkeit die auf sie gesetzten Hoffnungen in hohem Maße erfüllt und durch unermüdlichen Fleiß, rastlose Hingabe an die ihr zugeteilten Aufgaben. Die glänzenden Stimmmittel und die ungemein vorteilhafte äußere Erscheinung der p. Hiedler ließen es für die Königliche Verwaltung bisher wünschenswert erscheinen, die p. Hiedler von Fall zu Fall mit steigender Gage weiter zu verpflichten. (...) Ab 16. August 1896 zehnjähriger Vertrag mit 14.000 Mark im 1.-3. Jahr, 16.000 Mark im 4. und 5. Jahr und 18.000 Mark im 6.-10. Jahr, plus Spielgeld von 75 Mark, 80 Mal im Jahr garantiert." (Brief vom 27.5.1895 (Eingang 8.6., Antwort 15.6.)

64) Emil Stammer first worked as an actor in Riga (1876-86). After singing lessons he went to Königsberg where he performed in drama and opera. After a guest performance as Falstaff in Nicolai's opera in 1889 he went to Berlin and played mainly comic roles between 1889 and 1901 but also dramatic ones such as Wotan, Hagen, Commendatore, Sarastro, Osmin and Rocco. From 1903 to 1907 he performed at the Theater des Westens in Berlin and until 1922 in operetta. He also features in some silent movies. Stammer recorded for Odeon.

65) Franz Krolop had a most unusual career. He was born in Bohemia and studied law in Prague. After his degree in 1861 he worked for the military and finished as Oberstleutnant (Lieutenant Colonel). He left the army in order to study singing. He made his debut in Troppau (Opava) in 1863. From 1873 onwards he was an ensemble member in Berlin where he sang Rocco, Plumkett, van Bett, Figaro (Mozart), Leporello and other roles. After his sudden death Hochberg recalls in a letter of 22 June 1900: "Nach dem Tode Krolop's trat an mich die schwierige Aufgabe heran, für diesen ausgezeichneten Künstler einen geeigneten Ersatz zu finden ... "

66) Her debut was Azucena at the Kroll-Oper in Berlin in 1884. She was an ensemble member at the Königliche Schauspiele from 1892 to 1920. For a short time she became known as Goetze-Ritter (1859-1911). From 1901 onwards she recorded on G & T, Odeon and HMV (among others in the famous first recording of Gounod's *Faust* of 1908 as Siebel). There is also an Edison cylinder of 1905.

67) Sullivan wrote in his diary of 15 November 1895: "Production of 'Ivanhoe' very expensive . . ."

68) If any of these had remained after *Ivanhoe* was taken out of the repertoire after only ten performances, they were probably destroyed during World War II air raids.

69) Unfortunately cast members became ill during the run of *Ivanhoe*. Ms. Goetze was replaced by Henny Pohl for some performances and Mr Bulss (Templar) became ill early in December. The last performance was cancelled because of Mr Krolop's sudden hoarseness. Here the playbill had already been printed and it is strange that Krolop did not act on stage and somebody else sang from the score in the pit.

70) Jacobs, Arthur: *Arthur Sullivan*, Aldershot 1992 (second edition), p. 369. 70,000 Reichsmark was about double the amount of the annual income of the leading tenor, Eloi Sylva, who had a guaranteed sum of 36,000 Reichsmark.

71) See picture 41 in Saremba, Meinhard: *Arthur Sullivan – Ein Komponisten leben im viktorianischen England*, Wilhelmshaven 1993.

72) Not "kindlich" as transcribed in SASS booklet (child-like, positive; "kindisch" = childish, foolish; negative)

73) *Vossische Zeitung*, 27 November 1895.

74) The performances of Sullivan's *Ivanhoe* at the opera house of the Königliche Schauspiele in Berlin took place as follows: 26 November 1895 Berlin première; other performances: 29 November 1895 with Ms Pohl as Ulrica because of sudden hoarseness of Ms Goetze; 1 December 1895 with Ms Pohl; 4 December 1895 with Ms Pohl; [5 December 1895 "Marriage of Figaro" instead of "Don Giovanni" because of Mr. Bulss's hoarseness; the first signs of his declining powers]; 9 December 1895 *Mignon* instead of *Ivanhoe* because of Bulss's illness; 25 December 1895 with Ms Goetze as Ulrica; 26 December 1895 etc. as scheduled; 4 January 1896; 14 January 1896; 28 January 1896; 6 February 1896; 29 February 1896 *Bajazzi* and *Phantasien im Bremer Rathskeller*

instead of *Ivanhoe* because of Mr. Krolop's sudden hoarseness.

75) *Neue Zeitschrift für Musik*, 1 January 1896.

76) *Berliner Tageblatt*, 27 November 1895.

77) Count Hochberg took care of the orchestra and for the social needs of the musicians. In 1895 there were three levels of income between 1.500 and 3.000 Reichsmark. The orchestra was enlarged in the 1890s, among others with a third harp player, three more trombone players and two more horn players in 1895. Around 1900 the orchestra had: three leaders, 28 violin players, 10 violas, 11 cellists, 8 basses, 5 flutes, 5 oboes, 1 tuba, 5 trumpets, 2 percussionists and 3 harps.

78) *Neue Zeitschrift für Musik*, 1 January 1896.

79) *Neue Zeitschrift für Musik*, 1January 1896.

80) This included works by Lortzing, Nicolai, Auber and others.

81) The story of *Der Evangelimann* is as follows: Two brothers love the same woman, but the leading lady loves only the tenor. At the end of Act 1 a fire breaks out in the village. Mathias Freudhofer, the tenor, who wants to help put out the fire is suspected as being the fire-raiser, in consequence he is arrested and put in jail. The second act takes place thirty years later. After prison, Mathias has became an evangelist who now returns to his former village – but nobody recognises him. On the death bed his brother Johannes tells the supposed stranger that he had started the fire to destroy his brother's happiness and denounced him in court.

82) Sullivan's *Ivanhoe* the Berlin repertoire 1895/96:

November 1895

Date	Opera	Composer	Conductor
Fri 1	*Carmen*	Bizet	Felix Weingartner
Sat 2	*Fra Diavolo*	Auber	Felix Weingartner
Sun 3	*Hänsel und Gretel*	Humperdinck	
Mon 4	*Lohengrin*	Wagner	Carl Muck
Tue 5	*Die Hugenotten*	Meyerbeer	
Wed 6	*Der Evangelimann*	Kienzl	
Thu 7	*Das Rheingold*	Wagner	
Fri 8	*Die Walküre*	Wagner	
Sat 9	*Das Nachtlager von Granada*	Kreutzer	
Sun 10	*Fidelio*	Beethoven	Felix Weingartner
Mon 11	*Hänsel und Gretel*	Humperdinck	
Tue 12	*Carmen*	Bizet	Felix Weingartner
Wed 13	*Götterdämmerung*	Wagner	Felix Weingartner
Thu 14	*Der Evangelimann*	Kienzl	Carl Muck
Fri 15	*Allessandro Stradella*	Auber	Wegener
Sat 16	*Cavalleria rusticana/Das goldene Kreuz*	Mascagni/ Brüll	
Sun 17	*Lucia di Lammermoor*	Donizetti	Adolf Steinmann
Mon 18	*Die verkaufte Braut*	Smetana	
Tue 19	*Lohengrin*	Wagner	Carl Muck
Wed 20			

Sinfoniekonzert im Opernhaus:

Brahms: *Haydn-Variationen*;
Volkmann: *Serenade für Streichorchester*;
R. Strauss: *Eine symphonische Dichtung*;
Beethoven: *Eroica*   Felix Weingartner

Thu 21	*Die lustigen Weiber von Windsor*	Nicolai	Felix Weingartner
Fri 22	*Der Evangelimann*	Kienzl	Carl Muck
Sat 23	*Der Postillion von Lonjumeau*	Adam	
Sun 24	*Mignon*	Thomas	
Mon 25	*Die Tochter des Regiments*	Donizetti	
Tue 26	*Ivanhoe*	Sullivan	Carl Muck
Wed 27	*Der Evangelimann*	Kienzl	Carl Muck
Thu 28	*Der fliegende Holländer*	Wagner	Carl Muck
Fri 29	*Ivanhoe*	Sullivan	Carl Muck

Sat 30   **Sinfoniekonzert im Opernhaus**

Nicolai: *Kirchliche Festouvertüre* über *den Choral "Eine feste Burg ist unser Gott"*;
Brahms: *Violinkonzert*;
Resnicek: *Requiem*   Felix Weingartner

December 1895

Sun 1	*Ivanhoe*	Sullivan	Carl Muck
Mon 2	*Hänsel und Gretel /Die Puppenfee* (2:30 p.m.)		
	Zar und Zimmermann (7:30 p m)	Lortzing	Wegener
Tue 3	*Der Evangelimann*	Kienzl	Carl Muck
Wed 4	*Ivanhoe*	Sullivan	Carl Muck
Thu 5	Don Juan	Mozart	
Fri 6	Rienzi	Wagner	Carl Muck

Also in December 1895*:*

Der Ring des Nibelungen (complete); *Die Meistersinger von Nürnberg*; *Tristan und Isolde*.

In November & December 1895*:* Shakespeare at the Schauspielhaus (*Othello, Romeo und Julia, Richard II.*)

83) *Neue Zeitschrift für Musik*, 7 February 1900.

84) For details see: See: Saremba, M.: "In the Purgatory of Tradition – Arthur Sullivan and the English Musical Renaissance", in Brüstle, Christa / Heldt, Guido: *Music as a Bridge – Musikalische Beziehungen zwischen England und Deutschland*, Olms Verlag, Hildesheim/New York 2005, p. 33 – 71.

85) There were even publications such as Parry's "The Evolution of Music". This was a misunderstanding of Darwin, for whom evolution meant the adaptation of a species to the changing living conditions. In consequence there is a niche for everybody. Nevertheless Sullivan became irrelevant as he was regarded as old-fashioned.

86) Concerning a list of the orchestration of Sullivan's works see: Saremba, M.: *Arthur Sullivan*, Wilhelmshaven 1993, p. 140, or an updated version on the website www.sullivan-forschung.de

87) Interestingly enough, the Sullivan scholar William Parry stated in an interview: "I think it is very interesting to put Sullivan into context, not just with the other composers of the time but also in terms of the *artistic and*

cultural milieu that surrounded him. Clearly Sullivan was a *friend of* people like Millais, Byrne-Jones, who were the leading *Pre-Raphaelite* artists. Millais painted the gorgeous portrait of Sullivan that now hangs in the National Portrait Gallery. But there seem to me two other important links to the Pre-Raphaelite world: One might be Sullivan's approach to *orchestration* which seems to me very colourful, free of modern pigments, to be free of augmentation. And to that extent he seems to be almost like Pre-Raphaelites who were seeking to go back to a purer, more colourful, simpler time before Raphael, before the time when they thought that painting was ruined by modern influence. So Sullivan has got that aspect to him. But there is also the fact that he shares with the Pre-Raphaelites an *obsession with the medieval*, the dark ages, the middle ages. So in his great works such as *The Golden Legend, Ivanhoe, Haddon Hall, King Arthur* – there is this continued pre-occupation with that time when early English history was being created. The Victorians were incredibly keen on the dark ages and the medieval world from which Britain had emerged." (in the SWR radio series "Der englische Komponist Arthur Sullivan", by Meinhard Saremba, broadcast in June/July 2005).

88) Stanyon, Anne: *The Great Leeds Conspiracy: Sullivan, the 1898 Festival, and Beyond*, SASS Magazine No. 31 (winter 1990).

89) *Allgemeine Musik-Zeitung*, 30 November 1900. German obituaries in 1900 hardly mention *Ivanhoe*: In a very long obituary the *Neue Zeitschrift für Musik* (26 November 1900) just says: "Grand opera did not turn out to be successful. His first and only trial 'Ivanhoe' had its first performance at the so-called 'National English Opera House' but the work soon vanished from the programme." One short remark on *Ivanhoe* in 1900 (!) was that: "In the previous year [sic!] the work was performed for the first time in Berlin due to the order of the Emperor." Even in the early 20th century in some music publications writers picked on Sullivan. In a booklet by the publisher Reclam (who offers cheap libretto editions which are still popular today) a comment in an introduction to Marschner's *Der Temler und die Jüdin* mentions several *Ivanhoe* operas and writes about Sullivan that "in spite of the excellent production in Berlin . . . the score deserved that it failed completely". It is strange that there were no more stage performances, but the work was not completely forgotten in Germany's music literature. There were even some positive reactions towards *Die goldene Legende* and comments on *Ivanhoe* in a German opera guide of around 1913.

90) Wilhelm Kienzl: *Meine Lebenswanderung – Erlebtes und Erschautes*, Stuttgart 1926, p. 304 f.

91) Müllenbrock, Hans-Joachim: "Scott und der historische Roman", in *Die Neueren Sprachen*, November 1972, p. 664.

92) Original quotation: "Die Kunst gehört zu den ewigen Dingen, welche dieser toten Welt Leben einhauchen. ."

THE KNIGHT AND THE QUEEN

IVANHOE AND *GLORIANA*:

TWO NATIONAL OPERAS

By Martin Yates

Let's Make A National Opera

The received critical view of *Ivanhoe* is that it was an evanescent triumph - the first substantial opera by an Englishman to be genuinely popular with a paying audience, but like a rocket bursting magnificently, only to quickly wane and disappear. It was generally perceived to be an old-fashioned throwback to the English romantic operas of Balfe and Wallace, yet remained untouched by the all-pervading developments of Wagner and Verdi. It failed in its aim to establish an English style of opera, and had no significant progeny in the 20th century. Certainly its disappearance from the stage stopped all thought that it might ever be considered as a 'National Opera.'

But is this received view a fair assessment of the work and the aims of its composer?

Recently Jonathan Strong gave his opinion that the opera was a demonstration of a naturally English-language way of doing opera, and further regarded *Ivanhoe* as a seminal work whose significance was yet to emerge. ' . . . . I have always seen *Ivanhoe* as a pageant opera and a portrait opera. Its progeny in the 20th century are *Peter Grimes* and *Porgy and Bess*, the two best English-language operas of our era. All three focus on individuals, but in a distinct local context with a feel for the social movements of the times.' [1]

Clearly this assessment is vastly different to the received view and suggests that Sullivan was not far from the mark in writing a truly 'National Opera.'

Strong's reference to *Peter Grimes* brings forward the name of Benjamin Britten, the undoubted master of British opera, with *Grimes* being regarded as his unequivocal masterpiece. Yet Britten himself doubted that he had created in *Grimes* a truly 'national' opera, and six years later he embarked upon a work which he aimed would give the English stage an important national work to compare with the greatest of foreign models. How he set about creating this opera – *Gloriana* – and how the work finally emerged we can surely take as a definitive statement on how this master operatic composer viewed a 'national' work.

Sullivan also fully intended *Ivanhoe* to be a 'national' work – an expression of Englishness during a time when the operas of Wagner and Verdi had significantly changed the operatic landscape. So, surely, *Ivanhoe* too can be regarded as Sullivan's definitive statement on how an 'English' opera should be, and therefore both Sullivan's work and *Gloriana* are joined by a single aim: the creation of a truly national opera which expresses the core of 'Englishness.'

It will be seen, as this article progresses, that this single aim drew similar conclusions from both composers, and that the two works have much more in common than might be first imagined.

The Genesis of the Knight and the Queen

In order to fulfil their dreams of a truly national opera, both Sullivan and Britten turned to history – Sullivan responding to the Victorian taste for all things medieval, and Britten to the reign of the first Queen Elizabeth.

As early as 1885 Sullivan articulated his ideas as to how he wanted his opera to work: 'I apprehend that a successful (new) opera must be played every night to make money . . . . and for that you require a double cast of singers.' (2) This is exactly how *Ivanhoe* was played in the theatre. In an interview given to the *San Francisco Chronicle*, also in 1885, Sullivan explained how it would sound, avoiding the 'excesses' of the leading national styles:

> The opera of the future is a compromise. I have thought and worked and toiled and dreamed of it. Not the French school, with gaudy and tinsel tunes, its lambent light and shades, its theatrical effects and clap-trap, not the Wagnerian school, with its sombreness and heavy ear-splitting airs, with its mysticism and unreal sentiment; not the Italian school, with its fantastic airs and *fioriture* and far-fetched effects. It is a compromise between these three – a sort of eclectic school, a selection of the merits of each one. I myself will make an attempt to produce a grand opera of this new school. Yes, it will be an historical work, and it is the dream of my life. I do not believe in operas based on gods and myths. That is the fault of the German school. It is metaphysical music – it is philosophy. What we want are plots which give rise to characters of flesh and blood, with human emotions and human passions. Music should speak to the heart, and not to the head. Such a work as I contemplate will take some time. (3)

Sullivan saw English opera as a compromise, an agreement, a combination of these diverse elements, but without damaging the integrity of the whole. In other words the 'middle road.' That these ideals were expounded long before D'Oyly Carte suggested an inaugural work for the Royal English Opera shows how long Sullivan had been contemplating the work.

By the time he came to compose *Gloriana*, Britten's reputation was securely founded on several full-length works. The idea for the opera arose from a discussion between Britten, Peter Pears, and Lord Harewood:

> . . . . about nationalism in opera and its expression in typical operas of various countries. What about England? we wondered. We don't really have one. Well you'd better write one we said – and what better occasion than for the coronation (1953) . . . . (4)

Harewood's connection with the Royal family meant that a commission for Britten to write his 'National Opera' was soon obtained, and he was given a free hand to do what he liked. Thus he was able to respond to the stimulus of writing for an occasion – which he found an artistic boost – and also success would mean Establishment acclaim. Like Sullivan, Britten stood as an outside figure in the musical establishment of the time, and to both composers the writing of a significant national work would do much for their acceptance in critical circles.

In creating their operas both composers strove towards Englishness. Sullivan used English orchestral players and chose English-language singers, including some Americans. Britten wrote *Gloriana* with all the musical directions in English rather than Italian. He already had a core of English-language singers at his disposal at Covent Garden.

Taming the Book

Each opera is based on a novel: Scott's *Ivanhoe* and Lytton Strachey's *Elizabeth and Essex*. *Gloriana* is the only one of Britten's operas to be based on a novel. Both works clearly show their roots in the genre by their complex novelistic structure. The books needed to be condensed to make them effective for musical setting, and both Britten's librettist, William Plomer, and Sullivan's, Julian Sturgis, found that to use the best elements for a convincing story and operatic development, the framework for each opera had to include many different scenes.

Ivanhoe emerges in a three-act, nine-scene framework, and *Gloriana* with a similar three-act, eight scene framework. The scenarios of both are strategically planned to show contrasting plotting, the light and shade of the drama. In *Gloriana* the public and private worlds of the Queen are shown as fundamental to the dramatic structure. Similarly in *Ivanhoe* characters interact in the public arena – tournament, battle and execution – as well as having private and intimate scenes.

The novels also have numerous characters which needed to be introduced as part of the story. Both librettists had to omit several characters, like Francis Bacon and Sir John Harrington from *Gloriana* (though the Harrington character made a brief 'spoken' contribution at the end of the original version) and Athelstane and Front-de-Boeuf in *Ivanhoe*. Even so each work boasts over a dozen principal players and many lesser ones, with the result that some characters like Cuffe in *Gloriana* and Isaac of York in *Ivanhoe* appear rather perfunctory when compared with their more rounded counterparts in the novel. Some, like Locksley and Prince John in *Ivanhoe* and the ballad singer and the Recorder of Norwich in *Gloriana*, appear only in a small section of each opera. However these numerous characters add to the full picture being presented on stage, as do the numerous scenes.

The novelistic approach also leads to certain scenes in each opera being included even though they do not contribute to the dramatic thrust, but have to be there just to add another aspect to the story being related. This leads critics, who have woefully misunderstood the need to include these scenes, to suggest their irrelevance. In his review of the 1973 Beaufort Opera revival of *Ivanhoe* Winton Dean maintained that the song for Friar Tuck, 'Ho Jolly Jenkin,' was dramatically irrelevant, as was the whole scene in which it occurred. (5) *Gloriana* has also suffered in this respect with the Norwich Scene, which includes the choral dances, and the ballad singers scene, being particularly mentioned as irrelevant.

It is interesting that the film version of *Gloriana* by Phyllida Lloyd, who produced such a memorable revival in Leeds in 1994, omits three scenes – the Norwich, the garden scene, and the ballad singers scene. Regarding the loss of the Norwich scene, Lloyd wrote: 'I was sad not to have the music, but it doesn't contribute to the narrative thrust,' (6) This does not purport to be a film of the opera – more a study of the character of Elizabeth (and her singer) – but it does highlight how easily certain scenes could be omitted without disturbing the dramatic core of the opera.

However on stage all these scenes need to be included to satisfy the overall novelistic approach and to make a complete portrait of the period, as in *Ivanhoe*, or to show different facets of the Queen's character in private and public life, as in *Gloriana*. They are also included to 'flesh out' certain of the other characters in each opera. But this does highlight how difficult it is to convince critics who have a pre-conceived (i.e. post-Wagnerian) idea of how 'opera' works.

In the novels there are some situations that can be fully detailed in words, like the Tournament, or the siege of Torquilstone, or the rebellion of Essex and his followers. This is much more difficult to place on stage, and has led the librettists of each opera to use a dramatic device which, in Sullivan's case especially, has been derided: that of characters on stage describing events which are occurring off-stage. Modern audiences are familiar with this because the race scene in the musical *My Fair Lady* has the actors describing the race to the audience with a suggestive turn of the heads.

The device is used twice in both operas. The first time in both tournament scenes where in *Ivanhoe* the crowd describe the fight between the Templar and Ivanhoe, and in *Gloriana* Cuffe describes the scene to Essex. Later in this opera the ballad singer describes the progress of Essex's rebellion to the crowd on stage; at the siege of Torquilstone castle Rebecca describes to Ivanhoe the progress of King Richard and his soldiers. However in Sullivan's opera the action described off-stage does later come on-stage with thrilling effect.

The novelistic approach and effect on each opera also means that to differing degrees both operas need their audience to have a knowledge of the background to the characters and the historical situations so fully described in the novel.

As Britten's work is grounded in historical fact, a knowledge of Essex's past, for instance, adds more fully to the portrait shown in the opera and makes more sense of a line like 'Victor of Cadiz.' Andrew Porter wrote in 1953 'Composer and librettist have assumed a certain amount of knowledge in their audience.' He suggests that the audience read the libretto beforehand rather than not understand what is happening on stage. He concludes '. . . . . With *Gloriana* it would be better if they also read *Elizabeth and Essex*.' (7)

For *Ivanhoe*, especially in an age when the novel is less well known, it is useful for the audience to know about the 'age of unrest' which the novel portrays, and the hope of a Saxon restoration through Cedric's ward Rowena and the reasons why Ivanhoe has been disinherited. This is a problem neatly resolved in the recent Edinburgh performances by projecting information before each scene. (8)

The novelistic approach using lots of scenes and many characters can be seen in other 20th Century operas such as Vaughan Williams' *The Pilgrim's Progress* and Samuel Barber's *Anthony and Cleopatra*, and it leads to a suggestion of the tableau effect much admired by Russian composers, with Prokovief's *War and Peace* using the same formula on a bigger scale.

Jonathan Strong sums up the features by stating 'They are, in a sense, pageant operas, a series of finely-textured tableaux, not the relatively close-up psychological dramas of Verdi or Wagner, where a handful of characters hold our attention throughout.' (9)

A Song for Careless Hearts

When turning to discuss the musical settings of the operas, created with a distance of 60 years of tremendous change and upheaval, it is amazing that similarities of expression can be found. However it has to be realised as fact that both Sullivan and Britten were true men of the theatre, rare in British composers, who had a definite gift for writing opera, albeit of their own distinct and selected genre.

If one follows Alan Blyth's criteria for a true operatic writer, then each composer had the following in abundance:- ' . . . . in matters of construction, timing, pertinent orchestration, ideal allying of text and music and matching the 'tinta' of a score to the story in hand (c.f. Verdi) – in sum creating operas that work in the theatre.' (10)

Both composers were also established and successful in their chosen operatic fields long before they reached the works under consideration in this article, though it must be remembered that this was only Sullivan's second attempt at a fully through-composed opera. (11)

It is clear that both share a clarity and economy of expression and directness in the musical language. Sullivan once told Ethel Smythe, 'An artist has got to make a shillingsworth of goods out of a penn'orth of material.' (12) and Donald Mitchell wrote that Britten ' . . . . was famous for getting more portions from a roast than you'd have thought possible. It was the same sort of economy of mind he brought to writing music. Thrifty.' (13)

In Sullivan's case this economy emerged as a directness, even simplicity of style. In 1891 the *Athenaeum* wrote of *Ivanhoe* being a typical English Opera in subject, but also 'in the frank simplicity of nearly all the whole of the thematic material.' The 'extreme' simplicity of the vocal part-writing received more than its share of criticism, as did the unpretentiousness of the concerted music, either with or without chorus. Even the use of unison was condemned as pandering to 'ordinary listeners' and Sullivan was taken to task for taking the 'capacities of provincial companies into account when composing the opera.' (14)

Sullivan's directness of style – 'to have something to say and to say it as clearly as you can' (Matthew Arnold) – has always been seen as a problem, especially when viewed at the side of his illustrious contemporaries Parry and Stanford, whose excess of 'notes' on paper made their scores seem highly superior in comparison. However the sound world created by Sullivan is a world away from those academic exponents, and Sullivan carried the clarity and directness of his theatrical writing for the Savoy operas into *Ivanhoe*.

Amazingly in this context, Britten made the following comment about his writing in *Gloriana*: 'You know, the more simple I try to make my music, the more difficult it becomes to perform.' (15) (How many times has that been said when performing Sullivan's 'simple' music!) Donald Mitchell, to whom the comment was made, continues: ' . . . . . it is very relevant to *Gloriana*. *Gloriana* is, from one point of view 'simple', intentionally so, if by that one has in mind its directness of utterance, at which, I have no doubt, Britten worked particularly hard in this particular work.' Mitchell viewed the 'simple' part as being Britten's need to convey the 'period', the historic events in an historic period. The 'difficult' part, Mitchell continues, and to Britten the most challenging and interesting, was to convey the 'complex texture of conflicts, motives and ambitions.' (15) This 'difficult' part is seen as the

113

dramatic 'core' of the opera, and surely this also explains Sullivan's attraction to the similar elements – the humanity – in *Ivanhoe*.

In order to fulfil this 'simple' side Britten employs block harmony in the choral parts, especially the choral dances, and at several points does not disdain the use of unison – which the *Athenaeum* in 1891 regarded as giving ' . . . . a suggestion of vulgarity to those of more cultivated tastes.' However in the sound world created, the listener is unaware of any simplicity, just a feeling of clarity and directness which enhances rather than diminishes the music. (16)

Sullivan's response to the 'simple' and 'difficult' sides of his opera is shown not only in the varying of the musical texture, but primarily in his highly developed key sense. The more simple scenes are clothed in 'open' keys like C, D, G, or F majors, whereas the interior or more 'difficult' scenes employ the darker keys of Ab, Eb minor and Gb major. These are combined with a thicker texture in the written music, and in the fuller orchestration employed. A good example of Sullivan's developed key sense is by having the main key of the confrontation duet between Rebecca and the Templar – the Ab major/minor axis – echoed in the very first music they sing in the opera. The Templar's phrases are in Ab major and those of Rebecca in Ab minor.

Sullivan's perceptive use of a musical key for its expressive qualities has never been fully acknowledged, and in comparison *Gloriana* on the page looks positively less adventurous. Only at a couple of points, Essex's entry in Scene II and Penelope Rich's pleading in the Finale, does Britten use 6 sharps (F sharp major). For the rest of the opera the 'open' keys C, D, G and F predominate. Of course, the long tonal spans with which Britten builds his opera are infinitely more complex than they look on paper. Here again, as with Sullivan, how it sounds is a world away from how it is written.

But there are other areas in which the operas share common ground. Both Sullivan and Britten were consummate melodic composers who liked a 'good tune' and in each opera the vocal lines shine through clearly and directly, with word-setting beautifully placed to let the English language flourish. Even if their personal styles are very different – Britten writing vocal lines with a Purcellian mannerism – and Sullivan adopting a more naturalistic way, with less show – they both share an unrivalled skill in this area, and this is no doubt helped by the masterly transparent orchestral writing of each composer. For Sullivan this meant a world away from the heavy Brahmsian scoring of his contemporaries, and for Britten an openness and clarity with a bias towards the woodwind. In fact the size of the orchestra for each opera is very similar, except for the small stage band which Britten uses in the court scene.

Another hint that Britten was modifying his usual style in his 'national' opera was picked up by William Mann when he wrote that *Gloriana* was ' . . . a more diatonic and consonant opera . . . . than any he has yet given us: a great number of ideas are related through their common dependence on the notes of the triad.' (17) He could also be speaking of Sullivan, who throughout his works based many of his melodies on the triad. In *Ivanhoe* the Rotherwood theme, the Norman Knight motif and the many trumpet calls all owe their allegiance to the triad.

Old-Fashioned Numbers

Both operas contain elements that can be termed 'numbers' – detachable songs or arias that could lead an independent life outside the opera. In *Gloriana* this is more literally followed as within scenes different sections are actually numbered and named. For instance in Act II in the garden of Essex's home in the Strand, the pieces are: 1) Prelude & song; 2) Duet; 3) Double duet; 4) Quartet.

This dependence on a sequence of contrasted pieces suggests that Britten again had approached the writing of this opera differently from his previous works. Even though distinct 'numbers' can be found in *Peter Grimes* and *Billy Budd*, the tight symphonic intensity of those works is less evident in *Gloriana* even though the effect in performance is far from disjointed as their assimilation into the dramatic structure is seamless. However Peter Evans feels that ' . . . . in celebrating a great national occasion . . . .' Britten had ' . . . . slackened his customary control of those big musical spans which draw the listener more deeply into the . . . . drama.' (18)

Evans also suggests, quite interestingly in this context, that numbered and set pieces were used by Britten to give his audience a musical experience like that 'in the operas and operettas they might be expected to favour.' The detachable sections of the opera, like the Lute Song and the choral and courtly dances – all strongly evocative of the Elizabethan era – emphasise the impression of a tableau effect in the opera.

Writing 60 years earlier, Sullivan found himself closer in time to the Grand Age of the 'numbers' opera and the change wrought by Wagner in creating a 'seamless flow' of musical argument. In creating a 'national opera' for the future he needed to reconcile the past, which meant finding a solution to the most popular elements of the operatic form of the previous generation, full of set numbers and ballads. Also as Sullivan had stated his aim for 'Music as Drama' – that no halts in the music should allow for any kind of display he was rather tied as to what he could do in order to make a popular work. So despite creating a fast-flowing recitative and arioso, there are still many self-contained sections which could lead an independent existence away from the opera. This means several of these sections have full musical closures – pounced upon by Shaw as a weakness – and *Ivanhoe* began to be perceived as a 'numbers' opera and little else.

However the same 'numbers' and full musical closures are to be found in Britten's work, though some modern critics have excused this: 'the effect of musical closure is necessary where "music as music" has to be inserted into "music as drama." Essex's lute songs, the dances of the Norwich masque and of the court, the ballad singers extempore verses. It is these pieces, performed by or for the historical characters . . . . in some way suggest to us the Elizabethan period.' (18)

In the last scene of Act II, the ball at Whitehall, Britten achieved a memorable *coup de théâtre* when moving from 'music as music' – the courtly dances played by a stage orchestra – to 'music as drama' represented by the orchestra in the pit. How Britten achieved this has more than a suggestion of Sullivan's favourite device – the combination of two differing themes.

Here the 'Coranto' danced on stage and unison phrases from an earlier chorus, 'Victor of Cadiz' are combined. But slowly and imperceptibly the 'Victor of Cadiz' theme overwhelms the 'Coranto', and 'music as drama' is reinstated and the audience are now back in the reality of the opera. It is an astonishing moment in the theatre.

Although the double-chorus device is used in *Ivanhoe* – 'Fair and lovely is the may' – Britten's use has more of a suggestion of the chorus 'Tower Warders' in *The Yeomen of the Guard*, where the crowd's tune – with full harmony – is sung against the Yeomen's unison phrases. Britten adds a modern twist by having one theme in D major and the other in A minor.

If discussing 'music as music', then, at least three songs in *Ivanhoe* are excused for having a full musical closure because they are performed by one character to another – King Richard's 'I ask nor wealth', Friar Tuck's 'Ho Jolly Jenkin', and Cedric's drinking song in Act I. With other 'numbers' Sullivan hedges his bets and provides a slight pause before continuing the music, which leaves it open to a conductor as to whether or not he allows the audience to applaud. Rebecca's aria 'Lord of our Chosen Race' ends with a full close and a top Bb from the singer, something an audience find hard to resist. Surely in many cases in the opera this nod backwards is permissible!

In both operas full closures appear at the end of each scene. For Britten this was a departure from his usual practice, for in a work like *Peter Grimes* the music which links scenes – the so-called Sea Interludes (which incidentally also lead an independent existence away from the opera) are an integral part of the drama. To compensate for this lack of connection Sullivan links most of his scenes by key. Britten however starts each of his scenes in a different key.

Both composers begin each scene with a long orchestral introduction with musical elements which permeate the rest of the scene. This is most consistently followed by Sullivan in the Rotherwood and Copmanhurst scenes, but it is a particularly strong feature of every scene in *Gloriana*.

Ultimately it is Britten who is most consistent in integrating the elements of 'numbers' into the dramatic flow of his opera. For instance the courtly dances (which have been gathered together forming an independent group) are seamlessly integrated into the fabric of the dramatic action of the Court Scene, while the choral dances in the Norwich Scene are more of a self-contained tableau. Sullivan sometimes miscalculates the effect of 'numbers' as in the opening scene of Act III, where a slow aria for Ivanhoe – 'Come gentle sleep' – is followed by another slow one for Rebecca – 'Ah would that thou and I.' This causes a sense of hiatus in the dramatic pace, though it has to be said that both are then balanced by the extended dramatic sequence of the siege. At other times he is just as successful as Britten in integrating a 'number' in the dramatic flow. Writing of a BBC performance of a scene from the opera, Arthur Jacobs wrote: 'A long sequence from *Ivanhoe* not only confirmed the inner pathos of Rebecca's 'Lord of our chosen race', but showed Sullivan's skill in assigning it to its musical place within the gathering tension of the plot. (19)

In each opera the principle of autonomous 'numbers' is subtly modified by the use of key melodic phrases and motifs, which act as a unifying feature to connect dramatic contexts. The audience pick up on the inferences, used either vocally or in the orchestra, and associated with characters or situations.

Sullivan's extensive use of these musical and dramatic devices is discussed elsewhere, but Britten uses them in the same way in *Gloriana*. The 'Green leaves' chorus is the perfect example of a melodic phrase which is used again directly, or sometimes subtly modified and changed. Others can be noted, like the 'cares of state' phrase, or the 'Queen of my life' and 'the lion will fall' phrases. Britten uses them with a great deal more freedom than Sullivan, and with much more development, but basically the practice is the same.

The technique of using key melodic phrases and motifs certainly allowed each composer to view long spans in the dramatic structure of the musical scheme in each opera and thus mitigate the self-contained nature of 'numbers'.

How to Finish an Opera?

The finale of each opera not only represents a dramatic telescoping of events, but in its own way reflects the ethos of the era in which each composer was working. Both finales have encountered criticism; in *Ivanhoe* because Sullivan did not seem to deal adequately with the death of the Templar and Rebecca's sad fate, and Britten because at this point he uses spoken dialogue – seen as 'near to cheating' by William Mann. (17)

Each scene begins in a similar way with a sonorous chorus of male voices – the Templars (in G major) and Elizabeth's council (in Eb major) – both singing in unison phrases! In *Gloriana* Elizabeth hesitates to sign Essex's death warrant until she is enraged by the haughty pleading of his sister, Penelope Rich. This invention by Plomer was seen as a miscalculation because it makes the Queen look too capricious. (20) However she does so to a wonderful orchestral outburst playing the melody of 'Happy were he.' Then the stage darkens and the Queen's final moments are played out with spoken episodes and orchestral interjections. The opera ends with a hushed 'Green leaves' chorus, fading into silence. Again we can see how Britten repeats music heard earlier in the opera; and in Sullivan's finale too there is much music played which has importance elsewhere in the opera.

In *Ivanhoe* the death of the Templar, by an act of God, is also seen as a miscalculation. Sullivan doesn't seem to provide enough music for the Templar's fight (with Ivanhoe) and his death to be played out convincingly, and the pauses he does provide never sound long enough when not allied to stage action. In addition the romantic resolution is achieved without words as poor Rebecca, who loves Ivanhoe, is set aside in favour of Rowena. Sturgis originally gave Sullivan a more 'sombre ending', probably dealing more fully with Rebecca's fate, but it was changed and no copy exists. However it is inconceivable that Sullivan and Sturgis, writing for a popular audience, would have allowed a more 'sombre-ending' to the opera. Sullivan's final section, related in feeling to Rossini's wonderful ending to *William Tell* (though with fewer cymbal crashes!) is strengthened by the use of a musical phrase and the key of B major, from the Quartet 'Forgive thy son' first heard in the previous scene. This neatly points to the power of love and forgiveness. Certainly this final chorus sends the audience out on a high.

One of the criticisms of *Gloriana* was the very lack of this kind of quasi-Elgarian choral section to finish the opera. But it is just as inconceivable that Britten and Plomer, writing at that time, would have compromised their portrait of an aging queen with such a jingoistic feature, even to please a new Queen.

As they stand both finales perform better on stage than can be imagined from their look on the page. Surely this is all one can ask for an operatic score.

'Boriana' *'Gloriana'* and 'Botched' *Ivanhoe* (21)

The reception given to each work differed greatly. The Sullivan hit the mark fully! A great success which drew people to watch it several times, and ran for a full season of 6 months. This is exactly what Sullivan had envisaged and D'Oyly Carte had hoped for. However no other English operas were ready, and *Ivanhoe* was used to bolster up the season in November (1891), notching up a few more performances. The opera house then had to close, and was later sold. The failure of the scheme took the reputation of *Ivanhoe* with it, and the opera still suffers from the myths surrounding its demise.

Gloriana received its now legendary opening performances and, damaged by its notorious reception at the hands of the then British establishment, disappeared from sight until a new production in 1966 revealed it to be a powerful and stageworthy piece. It now accepted as one with Britten's other operatic masterpieces.

But did Britten succeed in his aim to create a truly 'National' opera? Writing about the fine Opera North production in 1994, Michael Kennedy was in no doubt:

> . . . . it can now be heard even more clearly that he 'did' compose a great national opera worthy of its occasion. It seems to me that by some alchemy the whole of English music is compressed into the haunting, evocative, melancholy melody 'Green leaves are we . . . .' We hear in it shades of Elgar and Vaughan Williams . . . . as well as Morley and Dowland. Whatever he may have thought of some of his elders and predecessors, Britten could not deny his birthright, and in *Gloriana* he consummated his relationship with past tradition. (22)

One could argue that Sullivan too consummated his relationship with previous generations in all his operatic works, with a synthesis of such models as the ballad operas of Shield and Dibdin and the romantic operas of Balfe and Wallace, and yet forged his own, albeit eclectic, style. In *Ivanhoe* he seems to be leading composers to a more English way of approaching the form – more middle-of-the-road, a 'compromise' of forms, yet a novelistic and naturalistic way which is very different to the trends shown by his contemporaries.

At the time English opera was definitely bogged down in influences from abroad, with operas either in the French style, as in Goring Thomas' *Esmeralda* and *Nadeshda*, or the Italian (Cowen's *Signa*), or the German 'Wagnerian' style as in *The Canterbury Pilgrims* by Stanford which was basically a *Meistersinger* copy, (even if he did use the tune 'Summer is a cumin in.')

Certainly Britten was aware of Sullivan's success in the theatre. He said of the Savoy Operas 'What heavenly shows these operas are!' (23) and he knew about the success of *Ivanhoe*: 'The Cambridge Circus opera house, for example, was built for Arthur Sullivan's *Ivanhoe*, which had an endless run of 155 performances.' (24)

This is not to suggest that Britten knew the music or that *Gloriana* is directly influenced by *Ivanhoe*. However we are still left with the impression that both Sullivan and Britten when pursuing their single aim came to the same conclusions as to how a national opera was to be written and how, more or less, it should sound.

Where *Gloriana* gains over *Ivanhoe* is that the character of Elizabeth is kept central to the dramatic core of the opera. It is she who dominates both dramatically and musically. Though this success is hardly surprising when viewing *Gloriana* alongside Britten's other major operas.

Sullivan, it must be remembered, had succeeded in an operatic form which needed a different kind of musical response, and *Ivanhoe* was a departure, for the first time in many years, from that response. It is obvious that he put a great deal of thought into what form the opera would take and despite much criticism recent performances have shown it, most definitely, to be stageworthy.

With *Ivanhoe* it is the novel itself that is the dominating force, not the single character of Ivanhoe, and this leads to a lack of dramatic focus throughout the opera which the listener does not feel when watching *Gloriana*. In this respect it is like Purcell's semi-operas, which have a pageant-like dramatic structure. (25) However despite these structural problems, the novelistic form chosen by Sullivan, and the way he clothed it in music, does now seem more modern than the operas of his contemporaries (and forward looking) and that Sullivan was not so far from the mark after all! Perhaps in the future *Ivanhoe* may indeed be regarded as an opera of seminal importance, and may gain for its composer the respect due for such a far-sighted work.

NOTES

'Let's make a National Opera' – the title is taken from Britten's work 'Let's make an opera' which is a play from which emerges the children's opera *The Little Sweep*. There is more than a whiff of Sullivan in this particular work!

1) Jonathan Strong: *Ivanhoe Explained*; Sullivan Society Magazine No 61, Winter 2005, p.20.

2) *Musical World*, 24 January 1885.

3) *San Francisco Chronicle*, 22 July 1885.

4) Lord Harewood: *The Making of Gloriana*; Opera Festival Edition, 2003. The operas discussed were *Boris* for the Russians, *The Bartered Bride* for the Czechs, *Carmen* for the French, *Aida* for Italy and, grudgingly on Britten's part, *Meistersinger* for the Germans.

5) Winton Dean, reviewing *Ivanhoe* in *Musical Times*, July 1973, p.722. The following letter from Nicholas Temperley, in response to Winton Dean, appeared in the *Musical Times*, September 1973, p.896:

Winton Dean claims in the review of *Ivanhoe* that 'this sort of romantic opera was a good 60 years out of date; so presumably was English taste'. This is the sort of thing that Fuller Maitland, Walker, Blom and other historians of English music have been saying for a long time. It is nonsense. Mr Dean seems to base his view on the fact that Sullivan did not use the methods of Verdi or Wagner. You might as well say that Verdi was out of date because he did not use Wagner's methods, or Wagner because he did not use Verdi's. If Sullivan had imitated one of them, his music would have been dismissed today as derivative. What he was trying to produce was a characteristically English type of opera which had existed, with varying success, since 1826. There was an audience for this form which was not the audience for Wagner or Verdi. The form continued to develop throughout the 19th century and *Ivanhoe* was a legitimate example of it. The fact that none of these works cuts much ice today does not indicate that they were out of date. Sullivan's opera was appropriate for its time — hence its success with public and critics. Only a critic with a thorough knowledge of its English predecessors is competent to judge its historical position.

Underlying Mr Dean's remark, and his whole review, is a more general assumption that every successful opera must show the kind of dramatic tension and character development that is found in Mozart or Verdi. One does not find much of it in *Orfeo* (Monteverdi) or Gluck, in Handel, or in Wagner. Yet critics persist in condemning lesser works on the bogus ground that they are not dramatic in this sense — perhaps because it is easier to analyse a story than a score. The fact is that audiences, past and present, have no difficulty in enjoying an evening of musical entertainment in the theatre even in the total absence of convincing drama. Certain schools of opera have flourished for long periods with only the most perfunctory dramatic framework, as Mr Dean well knows. English romantic opera was one of these. Audiences looked for a series of musical delights, each reflecting a simple emotion that was also well depicted on the stage. They also liked good acting, costumes and scenery. How these elements were 'worked up' into a plot was comparatively unimportant. I cannot see that there is anything immoral in this approach to opera. But if there is, it is too late to reform the audiences of the 1890s by lofty satire at their expense. I am still looking for a review that will criticize one of the rare revivals of Victorian opera on its own terms.

6) 'Radical Revision for TV *Gloriana*', *Gramophone*, December 1999.

7) Andrew Porter: '*Gloriana* and Lytton Strachey' in '*Gloriana* – A Symposium'; *Opera*. August 1953.

8) Revival of *Ivanhoe* by the Gilbert and Sullivan Society of Edinburgh, King's Theatre, Edinburgh, February 1999.

9) Jonathan Strong: 'Some Thoughts on *Ivanhoe*': Programme Note for the Boston Academy of Music performance of *Ivanhoe*, November 1991.

10) Alan Blyth: 'Britten's Genius'; letter to *Opera*, July 2005.

11) The first was *The Sapphire Necklace*, libretto by Henry Chorley, (Four Acts) 1864.

12) Ethel Smyth, quoted in Gervase Hughes, *The Music of Arthur Sullivan*, p.138.

13) Donald Mitchell: *Opera Now*, 1990.

14) *The Athenaeum*, 1891. Reproduced in Sullivan Society *Ivanhoe* booklet, 1990.

15) Donald Mitchell: 'The Paradox of *Gloriana*. Simple and Difficult', in: 'Britten's *Gloriana*', Aldeburgh studies in Music 1, 1993.

16) This question of simplicity of expression made its point recently when I discovered the vocal score of Jonathan Dove's 1998 opera *Flight*. It looked amazingly straightforward, with tunes and non-complex rhythmic patterns – especially when compared with, for example, Harrison Birtwhistle's complex operatic scores. However the sound world he creates for voice, and his wonderful orchestration, are a world away from the written page. I think this is especially true for Sullivan, where the printed vocal scores bear no relationship to the true sound created by the composer.

17) William Mann: 'The Vocal Score' in: '*Gloriana* – A Symposium, *Opera*, August 1953.

18) Peter Evans: 'Britten's celebration of musical Englishness'; Sleeve note for the recording of *Gloriana*, Argo Records, 1992.

19) Arthur Jacobs: *Arthur Sullivan – A Victorian Musician* (2nd Ed) 1992.

20) Andrew Porter: '*Gloriana* and Lytton Strachey'; *Opera*, August 1953.

21) The title is taken from the two most devastating opinions of each opera. 'Boriana' was the 'joke' overheard by Tony Mayer and printed in 'L'Affaire *Gloriana*', part of the Symposium in *Opera*, August 1953.

Reviewing Marschner's *Der Templer Und Die Jüdin* in *Opera*, January 1990, Rodney Milnes referred to Sullivan's work as '. . . botched, meretricious tosh . . . ' but forgot to mention that he had heard Marschner's opera in the revision made by Hans Pfitzner for Cologne in 1913, further revised for performance at the Wexford Festival, so that any comparison was irrelevant.

22) Michael Kennedy: 'A Great National Opera'; *Opera*, February 1994.

23) Britten's diary entry for Tuesday 29 November 1932. He had seen a performance of *The Mikado* at the Savoy. In December 1932 he listened to a BBC broadcast of *The Yeoman of the Guard* (his misspelling). He was also three times winner of the Sullivan Prize at the RCM.

24) Paul Kildea: *Britten on Music*, O.U.P. 2003, p.332. Britten could easily have heard the BBC broadcast of *Ivanhoe*, which took place in 1929, when he was aged 16.

25) A further analogy might be with a book-based musical such as *Pickwick*. The audience expects certain scenes to be presented on stage because they are familiar from the book, and judges the work in part on the way in which these scenes are managed.

GENERAL NOTE BY THE AUTHOR

My first experience of *Gloriana* was during the revival run in the late 60s, with Ava June playing the Queen. I gradually became aware that the opera was not so dissimilar from *Ivanhoe*, and the more I studied the more I realised that in aiming for a 'national' opera both composers had more or less reached the same conclusions. I make no apologies for discussing these two works or their composers, though for some readers the very mention of Britten and Sullivan together will be regarded as heresy. However I feel very strongly that a study of these two giants of British Opera is definitely an area ripe for exploration.

IVANHOE AND THE GRAMOPHONE

by STEPHEN TURNBULL

The story of *Ivanhoe* and the gramophone does much to destroy the myth of the opera's failure and disappearance, for recordings, although fewer since World War II, were numerous in the first forty years of the last century.

The number in *Ivanhoe* with the greatest popular appeal undoubtedly was, and remains, 'Ho! Jolly Jenkin'. [1] It is no surprise, therefore, that the earliest *Ivanhoe* recordings are of this song. The very first, by Tom Bryce, was made on 20 September 1898 on a seven-inch single-sided disc for Berliner; Bryce recorded the song again early the following month. Montague Borwell, who had made records of some G&S duets with the soprano Winifred Marwood in 1898, made a version of 'Ho! Jolly Jenkin' in November 1899.

In the following forty years or so more than sixty more recordings were issued, making 'Ho! Jolly Jenkin' the fourth most frequently recorded item by Sullivan in the 78rpm era after "The Lost Chord", "Onward, Christian Soldiers" and "Take a pair of sparkling eyes". [2]

William Paull, who played Cedric the Saxon in the 1895 Carl Rosa production of *Ivanhoe*, recorded the song for both Zonophone and the Gramophone Company. The latter, published in February 1902, the year before the singer's death, includes a clumsy discord in the piano introduction which, even in those days of limited quality control, should have led to a re-take. The Tuck in the Rosa production, A. S. Winckworth, published his "Ho! Jolly Jenkin" on the Favorite label in November 1906. Harry Dearth, who sang Tuck in the 1910 Beecham revival, recorded the song for the Gramophone Company (HMV), who published it three months after the performances. This particular recording, originally issued as a single-sided ten-inch disc, was later paired with Dearth's recording of the Drinking Song from *The Rose of Persia* and had a long life in the catalogue. Dearth also recorded the song for Odeon.

Sixty-odd versions of the same song must inevitably encompass a fair quotient of oddities, and "Ho! Jolly Jenkin" is no exception. Harry Thornton's version on the Encore label includes verse 1 only, and the side is made up with Violet Essex singing "Comin' thro' the rye" (the reverse side has two bell solos). Thornton recorded the song in its complete form for at least three other companies - Columbia, Pathé and Beka.

A single verse also found its way into a twelve-inch Columbia collection of 1937, "Great Bass Ballads" by Norman Allin. Although there is only piano accompaniment, this is one of the few recordings of the song to employ a chorus. The chorus makes an appearance on its own on a ten-inch Winner record of "Old and New", a pot-pourri of popular melodies by various composers arranged by Herman Finck; accompaniment is by the Scala Concert Orchestra. Finck's own orchestra (without the chorus) also recorded the selection for Columbia.

Genuinely strange, rather then merely odd, was "The Conundrum". The label of this 1911 single-sided twelve-inch HMV disc posed the following conundrum:

I'll make you languish, or I'll make you laugh;
I'll stir your blood or I'll make you dance.
What am I?

The listener was invited to provide the answer by placing the needle on the record, which would then play, at random, one of four tunes: Guy d'Hardelot's "Because", "I want to sing in opera", "Grizzly bear rag", or a rendition by Robert Radford of verse 2 of "Ho! Jolly Jenkin."

But surely the most curious of all was the ten-inch HMV disc issued in 1917 of the piano accompaniment alone. Something like twenty songs were treated in this early experiment in karaoke, and it is indicative of its popularity that "Ho! Jolly Jenkin" should be one of them.

Perhaps the most distinguished singer to record "Ho! Jolly Jenkin" was the great Australian bass-baritone Peter Dawson, who made an Edison cylinder of the song around 1904 at the very outset of his career. As far as is known Dawson never revisited the song, although in 1922 he made a recording of Sir Brian's "Woo thou thy snowflake" on a twelve-inch HMV plum label disc. Robert Radford had recorded this aria in 1915 on a ten-inch Zonophone Celebrity record. The reverse side was "Ho! Jolly Jenkin", complete this time. (3) Harry Dearth also recorded both numbers ("Woo thou thy snowflake" for Odeon), as did David Bispham (for Columbia in 1909 and 1910) Other distinguished singers who recorded "Woo thou thy snowflake" included Frederick Austin, Roy Henderson and the famous Scots baritone Andrew Black, who had often worked with Sullivan and frequently appeared as Lucifer in *The Golden Legend*. Bispham did in fact sing the confrontation scene between Rebecca and the Templar under Sullivan's direction at the Leeds Festival of 1895.

The Beecham *Ivanhoe* led to another interesting recording. In 1916 Edith Evans, the Rowena in that revival, recorded Rebecca's "Lord of our chosen race" for HMV, with an orchestra conducted by Percy Pitt, conductor of the Beecham performances. In the same year a version of Ivanhoe's "Come gentle sleep", with orchestral accompaniment conducted by Hubert Bath was issued, also by HMV. (4) Ivor Walters had recorded the song for Pathé two years earlier.

Band and orchestral selections from operatic works were a staple of the record companies' catalogues in the era before long-playing records. Sullivan's operas had always been popular fare in this format and consequently a number of *Ivanhoe* selections were issued. Perhaps the best known, and certainly the most substantial, is the twelve-inch double-sided Columbia disc by the Band of the Grenadier Guards conducted by Captain George Miller, issued in July 1929, shortly after the BBC radio broadcasts of the opera. 1929 also saw a new recording of "Woo thou thy snowflake" by Arthur Fear.

The era of microgroove recordings proved to be less kind to *Ivanhoe*. The immediate postwar years were barren, but the 1970s and the beginnings of the Sullivan revival brought some improvements. George Baker's 1927 HMV recording of "Ho! Jolly Jenkin" achieved an LP reissue in 1970 as part of a tribute to the singer. *Donald Adams Sings Sullivan and Gilbert* was a live recording of a recital given by the singer in Los Angeles in 1971, including a performance of "Ho! Jolly Jenkin". (5) The following year same singer was joined by Sylvia Eaves, Thomas Round and John Cartier for the Act III quartet "Forgive thy son" on a Pearl LP of Sullivan rarities. Sylvia Eaves sang "Lord of our chosen race" on the same disc. The orchestra was conducted by Peter Murray.

The first complete *Ivanhoe* appeared in 1974 on three LP records. Issued by Rare Recorded Editions, the recording was made live at performances of an amateur production of the opera by Beaufort Opera in 1973 and suffers from all the faults inherent in a live recording. Although it was welcomed by enthusiasts at the time of its issue, the welcome was very much on the basis that anything was better than nothing, for the standards of performance are no more than moderate (in some places the singing is execrable) and the records made a poor case for *Ivanhoe*. Nevertheless, the recording had the dubious honour of being 'pirated" by an American company in 1982.

In 1986 the Sir Arthur Sullivan Society opened negotiations with the Prince Consort of Edinburgh to make a complete recording of *Ivanhoe*. The Consort, whose previous live recordings of *The Emerald Isle*, *The Beauty Stone* and *The Rose of Persia* had been issued on LP by Pearl, set about assembling the best possible cast and orchestra. The singers included Irene Drummond, Frances McCafferty, Bruce Graham and the Consort's co-director Alan Borthwick in the title role; the conductor was David Lyle.

Rehearsals began in August 1987 and the recording was made on four Sundays in November and December. The master tapes were formally handed to the Sullivan Society in March 1988 and, after editing and mixing, the opera was issued on three Pearl compact discs in November 1989. The total cost of the project, some £4,500, although paltry by commercial standards, represented a huge financial commitment by the Society at that time. The recording was well received by critics and listeners alike, and won the 1990 Best Opera Recording award of the Music Retailers' Association. (6)

The compact disc era has seen further additions to the available *Ivanhoe* recordings. In 1991 Pearl issued a CD of transfers from the author's collection of Sullivan 78s. Entitled "Sir Arthur Sullivan: Sacred and Secular Music" this included Roy Henderson's 1925 recording of "Woo thou thy snowflake", a 1930 "Ho! Jolly Jenkin" by Bernard Dudley and the 1929 Columbia selection. The following year, a CD from Symposium to mark the 150th anniversary of Sullivan's birth, reissued three more *Ivanhoe* items: Bispham's "Ho! Jolly Jenkin", Dawson's "Woo thou thy snowflake" and Evans' "Lord of our chosen race".

In 1998 the Sullivan Society's disc *Sullivan and Co.* was issued by TER. This contained selections from all Sullivan's late operas specially recorded at EMI's famous Abbey Road Studios in London. *Ivanhoe* was represented by "O moon art thou clad" sung by Valerie Masterson and "Ho! Jolly Jenkin" sung by Gareth Jones and the chorus. The National Symphony Orchestra was conducted by David Steadman. A 2000 disc of English Victorian opera arias, *The Power of Love*, by the Australian soprano Deborah Riedel, contains mostly material by Balfe and Wallace but includes "Lord of our chosen race". The Australian Opera and Ballet Orchestra is conducted by Richard Bonynge. A major milestone will be reached in 2009 when the opera will be recorded complete by Chandos under Richard Hickcox.

NOTES

1) There is a most amusing account in a recent issue of the *Daily Telegraph* of a vocal academy for bullfinches which has been started in Covent Garden market. Just at the present moment it seems that there is a lively demand for piping bullfinches, and the writer gives an interesting description of the process of training. The birds are taught by a small hand reed organ, which is kept going all day long.

One is shortly expected to make its debut with the "Bogie Man," but the coming bird is that which is engaged on "Ho! Jolly Jenkin." Unluckily it takes some eighteen months to complete the musical education of a bullfinch in a tune, so that they never can be quite "up to date!" . . . . . According to the writer in the *Daily Telegraph*, they have all the *minauderies* of a *prima donna*, and watch their audience most carefully while they are performing. We may quite expect to see the whistling lady superseded in the coming season by the piping bullfinch. *Musical Times*, 1 June 1891, p.334.

2) It is impossible to give exact numbers because records are still being discovered, but there were around 65 recordings of "Ho! Jolly Jenkin" in the 78 era, compared with around 120 of "Take a pair of sparkling eyes", more than 150 of "Onward, Christian soldiers" and about 400 of *The Lost Chord*.

3) The Gramophone Company had taken over the British Zonophone Company in 1903 and thereafter used Zonophone as its "budget" label.

4) These two recordings, along with David Bispham's "Ho! Jolly Jenkin" and "Woo thou thy snowflake", were included by Pearl in a compilation LP *Sullivan Without Gilbert* on their Opal label in 1986.

5) Reissued on CD by Musical Collectables in 2006.

6) The award was shared with Jessye Norman's recording of *Carmen*. Alan Borthwick and David Lyle's involvement with *Ivanhoe* continued: in 1999 the Gilbert and Sullivan Society of Edinburgh marked its 75th anniversary with a week's fully staged run of the opera at the King's Theatre, Edinburgh, directed by Alan Borthwick and conducted by David Lyle. A live video recording was made and sold non-commercially by the Society.

THE BBC BROADCAST OF *IVANHOE* 1929 – *Radio Times*, Wednesday 27 March 1929 p.713

' Ivanhoe '

A Romantic Opera in Three Acts
Words adapted from Sir Walter Scott's Novel by
Julian Sturgis
Composed by
ARTHUR SULLIVAN

The Wireless Symphony Orchestra
Leader, S. Kneale Kelley
The Wireless Chorus
(Chorus-Master, Stanford Robinson)
Conducted by
PERCY PITT

Relayed from the Parlophone Studios
By *courtesy of The Parlophone Company*

Cast in order of appearance :

Cedric	STUART ROBERTSON
Isaac, of York	ROBERT EASTON
De Bracy	HARDY WILLIAMSON
The Templar	LEYLAND WHITE
Rowena	INA SOLEZ
Ivanhoe	WALTER WIDDOP
Friar Tuck	ROBERT EASTON
King Richard	FRANKLYN KELSEY
Prince John	ROBERT CHIGNELL
Rebecca	STILES ALLEN
Locksley	CAVAN O'CONNOR
Ulrica	LONDA SEYMOUR
Grand Master	ROBERT CHIGNELL

Narrator, Mr. FILSON YOUNG

THE BEECHAM REVIVAL OF *IVANHOE* 1910

IVANHOE! How thick and fast the memories come back to those old enough to recall all that the success of Sullivan's *Ivanhoe* and of the house in which it was produced was intended to mean in the cause of national British opera. In the nineteen years that have elapsed what changes have we not seen in things operatic. How we all thought and prayed then that Sullivan's success meant permanent success – that at last we had attained to the haven where we would be, that British opera was henceforth to be a living force, that Sullivan, the master of an entirely individual style, had at length laid the solid foundation which so often before had been laid upon the shifting sands. Nineteen years have gone, and are we in reality very much nearer the aforesaid haven if the facts be faced fairly and squarely, now than then? Not so near, some will say. Certainly no British grand opera has "run" in the meanwhile for 160 nights — the span or *Ivanhoe*'s original existence. But one opera does not make for permanent salvation in things operatic, and we all know now — it is very ancient history — that it is futile to attempt to found a national opera upon one work, however distinguished that work may be.

Still — 160 nights! How many operas that have been composed since *Ivanhoe* can count so many performances. Not, probably, a great many. It was good, then, that D'Oylv Carte's worthy successor, Mr. Thomas Beecham – if so he may be described — should include this work in the admirable season now in progress at Covent Garden. And it is significant that during the same all too brief season places should be found in the scheme for works as dissimilar as *Ivanhoe* and *Elektra*, the one a triumph of a day that may or may not be dead, the other the triumph of the temperament of today. For the genuine opera-lover it is all to his advantage to renew his youth, as it were, by witnessing performances of the works that appealed when he was twenty years younger. Not one such opera-lover – at least, of ordinary intelligence — will scoff at *Elektra* because its methods are not those employed in *Ivanhoe*. Nor will he think the less of Sullivan's, one grand opera because of its complete dissimilarity from Strauss's latest work. But he may fail to note that each of these operas is in a sense a landmark, and that in spite of the wide-reaching and essential differences between them, they have this in common, that each is thoroughly characteristic of its composer, and each is stamped indelibly with its creator's individuality. Other times bring not only other manners and customs, but also methods that are the direct outcome of what may be called evolution. If for no other reason than that in reviving *Ivanhoe* now, when *Elektra* is ringing in everyone's ears, Mr. Beecham has provided a perfect historical object lesson; he has earned a very special meed of praise from those who possess the historic sense.

But, in a sense, this is only half the truth. No doubt whatever that a good deal of the original gold in *Ivanhoe* has become tarnished in the passage of time; it is in the very nature of things that this should be so in all but the greatest art-work. Nevertheless there remains still a residue of mellifluous gold — such as the ballad 'Ho, Jolly Jenkin' which the gallery vociferously redemanded last night — which shines as effulgently now as before. That which tells the tale of time's passage most explicitly is the constant and rather irritating habit of the librettist in sub-dividing his scheme into innumerable scenes, whereby the connecting thread of the tale he would tell apt is to be broke. This fault — from a present-day point of view — renders the libretto decidedly weak, and its weakness reacted upon the composer, who alone was obviously unable to carry forward the narrative, so to say, and in consequence his music seems at times to lose its point. But when all is said that can be said, Arthur Sullivan created tunes that have passed, as it were, into the language – and few of our native composers - few indeed! — can say so much. For this reason, as for others referred to, it will always be a pleasure to hear his music, for if his aim was not of the loftiest, it certainly was well directed, and no composer has given to the public more of himself, for none could do so.

The piece was superbly and most picturesquely staged — whether a mere ante-room or the lists at Ashby, the storming of the castle, or what-not be in question — and the greatest credit is due to the unnamed "scenic artist" who was responsible. No pains, clearly, had been spared in re-presenting the work. Moreover the performance under Mr. Percy Pitt was on the whole a good one. True, those of us who own a somewhat hoary memory were not often called upon to wipe clean our memory-tablets. But both the Misses Perceval Allen and Edith Evans as Rebecca and Rowena; Mr. Walter Hyde, an entirely admirable Ivanhoe; Mr Robert Maitland, a competent Templar; Mr Harry Dearth, a sufficiently – perhaps too sufficiently – low comedian Friar Tuck; Mr Kaufmann, a bustling King Richard; and the rest – the cast is of great length – all did that that in them lay for the benefit of a native composer. And in this they succeeded beyond ordinary anticipations, for the majority of them have been, it seems, brought up in a school that is far removed from the suave-simplicity school of Sullivan. It is pleasant to record that there was an enormous audience, which was nothing if not enthusiastic, for calls and recalls were abundant. *Daily Telegraph*, 9 March 1910.

ACT 3 SCENE 3 - REBECCA AT THE STAKE

Illustrated Sporting And Dramatic News, **19 March 1910**

SCENE FROM *ROBIN HOOD* – *Illustrated Times* 27 October 1860

SCENE FROM *LURLINE* – *Illustrated Times* 3 March 1860

MACFARREN'S *ROBIN HOOD*

By David Eden

In the course of his review of *Ivanhoe* George Bernard Shaw remarks that Sullivan's score does not represent 'in any essential point' an advance on *Robin Hood* by George Macfarren (1807-1887), written in 1860. (1) Shaw had seen a performance of *Robin Hood* at the National Standard Theatre in Bishopsgate in 1889, saying on that occasion that it was no better than Cellier's *Doris*. (2) Authorised by such insights from the Boris Johnson of music criticism, a glance at *Robin Hood*, if not *Doris*, may perhaps be justified as an aid to the understanding of Sullivan's work.

Macfarren, who became blind during the composition of *Robin Hood*, composed several stage works at the beginning of his career. He was knighted at the same ceremony as Sullivan and was held in esteem by the latter, who, at a Leeds rehearsal for *King David* in 1883, said 'I wonder where the old man gets such beautiful ideas.' (3) Macfarren's first effort, an operetta called *Genevieve, The Maid of Switzerland*, was produced in 1834. It was followed by *The Devil's Opera* (1838), *An Adventure of Don Quixote* (1846), *King Charles II* (1849) (4) and *The Sleeper Wakened* (1850). (5) *Robin Hood*, to a libretto by John Oxenford, represents a departure inasmuch as it was conceived – and received – as a specifically 'English' opera.

In 1860, for reasons best known to himself, the theatrical impresario E.T. Smith decided to found what he called the Grand Coalition Opera – 'a scheme for running Italian and English opera on alternate nights at popular playhouse prices.' (6) Her Majesty's Theatre, of which Smith was already lessee, was chosen, and a distinguished group of singers engaged – Theresa Tietjens and Antonio Giuglini for the Italian opera (*Il Trovatore*); Helen Lemmens-Sherrington, Charles Santley and Sims Reeves for the English rival. The avowed purpose, according to the *Morning Chronicle*, was 'sustaining the fortunes of national English opera, the establishment of Italian opera being an afterthought.' (7)

Smith's intention was to open on Monday 8th October 1860 with *Robin Hood*. In the event *Robin Hood*, conducted by Charles Hallé, was not seen until Thursday 11th, when it received rave notices, including the following: 'The greatest work that has been produced for the English stage since the days of Purcell,' and '. . . the championship of the English school, until a better opera than *Robin Hood* is produced, must remain with its composer.' (8) So successful was Macfarren's work that *Il Trovatore* itself was cast into the shade, being replaced with, successively, *Don Giovanni, Lucrezia Borgia* and *Les Huguenots*. Unfortunately for English opera, the Pyne-Harrison production of Wallace's *Lurline* at Covent Garden was also threatened. 'It was,' said a wag, 'less *Robin Hood* than robbin' Harrison.' (9)

Robin Hood ran for three nights a week until 15 December, after which Smith replaced it with a pantomime, *Harlequin and Tom Thumb*. Following the poor success of *Tom Thumb* he produced *The Bohemian Girl* on 21 January 1861, and revived *Robin Hood* on 5 February. *Fra Diavolo* replaced *The Bohemian Girl* on 15 February, both operas running in tandem with *Robin Hood*, which continued to be performed three times per week. (10) The final night of *Robin Hood* fell on 23 February, making a grand total of 37 performances. On 28 February Smith produced Wallace's *The Amber Witch*, with indifferent success. According to Charles Santley there was no attempt at stage management, either for *The Amber Witch* or *Robin Hood*: 'we all wandered on and off and about the stage as we pleased.' (11) *Robin Hood* was next given by the Pyne-Harrison company at Covent Garden on 8 November 1861 when it alternated with *Lurline* and Howard Glover's *Ruy Blas* for a total of 5 performances, ending on 22 November 1861. (12) On 30 November Pyne-Harrison produced Balfe's *The Puritan's Daughter*. It is noteworthy that the English operas which were so conspicuously unavailable to D'Oyly Carte in 1891 were apparently in abundant supply in 1861

In spite of its success *Robin Hood* seems to have fallen silent until 28 June 1879, when it was performed at the Alexandra Palace. This performance was organised by J.W. Turner, whose Grand English Opera Company was responsible for the performances in 1889, when Bishopsgate was temporarily raised to national prominence by the visit of *Corno di Bassetto*. On this occasion *Robin Hood* received three performances in company with *Maritana* and *The Bohemian Girl*. (13) Turner's production was also seen at the Princess's Theatre in August 1889. (14) No doubt other performances remain to be traced.

Contemporary accounts leave no room for doubt that *Robin Hood* was regarded as a fresh departure for English opera, both as to words and music. *The Times* praised the libretto as one 'with which a musician capable of doing anything is pretty sure to do his best.' (15) *The Morning Chronicle* was of the opinion that a new dawn had come:

> The success achieved by the new opera *Robin Hood* is likely to exercise a powerful influence on the fortunes of the national dramatic music of England. For a dozen years and more the English public has been held bound in the thralls of two composers, natives of the Emerald Isle, Messrs M.W. Balfe and Mr W.V. Wallace, and managers and publishers have turned a deaf ear to solicitations from any other quarter for the production of new works. *The Bohemian Girl* and *Maritana* – how, it would be difficult to discover – became models for future operatic writers, and any deviation from the style of such acknowledged masterpieces was regarded as an act of temerity if not of folly. The mawkish sentimental school, which one of the two Hibernian composers originated, and the other corroborated and improved upon, making it more lachrymose, like a minor seventh the common chord, became the rage, and all other kinds of music on the stage ignored. The tearful lyrics and labyrinthine mode of expression adopted by Mr Alfred Bunn and other native bards, whose names will occur to every reader, no doubt tended largely to establish the new school. The words, too subtle and profound for vulgar apprehension, were referred to depth of feeling, and what the musician could not understand he tuned to melancholy. The singers, too, especially tenors, found great account in these vocal lamentations, and turned their whole attention to sighs, groans, tears, misery and despair. "Broken Hearts" and "eternal separation" were the bells on which poets and musicians rang the changes *ad infinitum*; and Music, with dishevelled hair, loosely clad, and a pocket handkerchief to her eyes, went slowly and solemnly through the land crying aloud, "Who'll weep with me?" . . . . .

> That Mr Macfarren was as anxious about the poetry as the music is plain, from his engaging Mr Oxenford to write the libretto of *Robin Hood*, the hearing of which, after the miserable trash we have been compelled to listen to for years, comes like a breath

from heaven after inhaling noxious gases from polluted stews. Mr Oxenford is a true poet, and the book of *Robin Hood* is true poetry, and constitutes even a greater change from the concoctions of Messrs Fitzball and Harris, than Mr Macfarren's music from that of the Hibernian Brothers. . . . . .

When a new work for the stage was announced by the composer of *Charles II* and the cantatas *May Day* and *Christmas*, nothing short of a masterpiece was expected, nor has expectation been disappointed. Mr Macfarren's *Robin Hood*, indeed, is a work of which English musicians may be proud, and England itself need not be ashamed. Judging from his two last dramatic works it would appear that the composer's principal aim has been to give English music in true English colours, and to borrow nothing from foreign sources. This was in itself a novel idea and a violent departure from that style, or, more properly, no style, of which *The Bohemian Girl* and *Maritana* are such striking examples. That Mr Macfarren has invariably caught the old English tone and feeling, we will not say, nor that sometimes he has not sinned in marrying modern instrumentation to antiquated melody. But these are questions hardly to be mooted in this place. The consideration whether the music be good or not – more to our immediate purpose – may be settled in a word. We may, without hesitation, affirm that *Robin Hood* is the most masterly and complete work of an Englishman ever heard on the English stage. That this is saying a good deal will be acknowledged when it is remembered that in the list of English composers are included the names of Dr Arne, Purcell, Henry Bishop, Barnett, Hooke, Balfe, Wallace and others. (16)

Turning from such praise to the actual work one hardly knows how much disappointment to expect. In John Oxenford's version of the story Marian is the daughter of Sir Reginald de Bracy, the Sheriff of Nottingham. She is in love with Locksley, who is none other than Robin Hood in disguise. After a number of vicissitudes in the greenwood and at the butts Locksley is recognised by the dastardly Sompnour and captured. Awaiting execution, he is reprieved at the last minute by King Richard provided he forswears his *alter ego* and serves him, Richard, in future. The lovers are united with the blessing of the Sheriff, who is unexpectedly endowed with sympathetic qualities. The libretto, in three acts and eight scenes, includes passages of speech and makes no attempt to do anything other than tell a familiar tale as economically as possible. Oxenford's natural ability produces an occasional felicitous turn of phrase, but nothing is done to introduce emotional or dramatic complexity into a legend that resists such treatment. From a later perspective most interest attaches to a game of Blind Man's Buff played at the Fair outside Nottingham (Act II Scene III):

A round dance by the peasants. Tilting at the quintain. "Hoodman Blind."

CHORUS: Who's for a game of "Hoodman Blind?"

Let him come here, and his eyes we'll bind.

Now, catch whom you can, Sir Hoodman Blind.

Turn round three times –

Don't be afraid,

Some pretty maid

Will gladly be caught if catch her you can.

The Sompnour, entering disguised as a mendicant friar, is caught by the blinded peasant girl.

CHOR: You're caught! You're caught!

SOMP: Rude hussies, for shame!

                   Behave as you ought.

CHOR: 'Tis the rule of the game. (17)

The Times described the music of the 'Hoodman Blind' scene as 'a piece of concerted music almost worthy to be ranked as a finale.' The *Morning Chronicle* was impressed by 'The grand scena "Hail, happy morn!" in the second act', which was '. . . evidently written after the manner of *Agatha's* scena in *Der Freischütz*. It has the same situation, and involves exactly the same mental emotions. That Mr Macfarren has not plagiarised a bar, and that his beauties are all his own, cannot be denied. The florid passages in the allegro are extremely telling . . .' Elsewhere the trio "By all the love that you have shown me" is regarded as 'one of the most masterly and powerful compositions in the whole work,' while the partsong "The wood, the gay green wood," 'is perhaps the most original piece in the opera.' 'The two long scenes in the second act – that wherein the outlaws rob the Sompnour and make him dance, and the entire scene of the fair at Nottingham – are inimitable throughout.' However a long scena for the Sheriff, "My child has fled," is regarded as a mistake: 'Nobody has any sympathy for the Sheriff . . . . his moans therefore do not excite interest, nor are his expressions of vengeance heeded. The scena has magnificent points. The andante is almost torturing from its intensity of feeling, but the grand descriptive wind-up cannot be appreciated by the generality of listeners.' (18)

In spite of the concerted music the opera as a whole is dominated by the songs. The *Athenaeum*, altogether less impressionable than other journals, pointed out that '. . . every English opera must have *the* ballad for the tenor – and the shops.' (19) The tenor ballad lives on conspicuously in *The Sorcerer* and *The Yeomen of the Guard*; but if we are looking for comparisons with *Ivanhoe* then the contemporary stress on the 'Englishness' and 'simplicity' (20) of Macfarren's score suggest that Sullivan was deliberately working in a tradition, and one moreover which had no choice but to take account of 'the generality of listeners.' Macfarren uses a (very) simple song for Marian, 'True Love', as a recurrent theme throughout the opera when Marian is involved. This suggests that Sullivan's similar practice in *Ivanhoe* may be an 'English' homage to Macfarren as much as a step in the direction of Wagner. (21) On the other hand the musical style of 'True Love' is the kind of thing Sullivan reserved for the drawing room – there is nothing so elementary in *Ivanhoe*. In the last resort Sullivan outdistances Macfarren completely. The great colloquy between Rowena and Ivanhoe (Act I Scene 2) and the dramatic interview between Rebecca and the Templar (Act II Scene 3) are music of adult emotional significance not found in English opera since Dido's Lament. The same is true of many other passages. One is tempted to conclude that *Corno di Bassetto*, his critical faculties damaged beyond repair by devotion to Wagner's impersonal chthonic ponderosities, simply failed to understand Sullivan's more natural approach to humanity. Quite possibly he was too fond of his own jokes to care.

ILLUSTRATIONS

The scene from *Robin Hood* belongs to the final act, when Marian realises that Robin is Locksley. She falls back, with her head oddly displaced. The scene from *Lurline* shows Lurline's cave at the bottom of the Rhine. Lurline has presented her lover, Count Rudolph, with a magical ring. However his former fiancée, Ghiva, seizes the ring and tosses it into the Rhine, where it is retrieved by the gnome Zeelick. The illustration shows Ghiva seizing the ring immediately before throwing it into the Rhine. *The Amber Witch* is set in Pomerania. Mary, a young woman who collects amber, is accused of witchcraft. She is saved from being burned at the stake by Rudgier, her beloved. The illustration shows the moment of rescue.

NOTES

1) Shaw, *Shaw's Music*, p.258.

2) Shaw, *Music in London*, p.107.

3) Banister, *George Alexander Macfarren*, p.309.

4) *King Charles II* is not a dignified work, involving as it does the comic misadventures of the merry monarch at the King's Head tavern in Wapping. It does however include a madrigal, 'Maidens would ye scape undoing,' described by Banister (p.196) as 'worthy of a place beside the finest madrigals of Wilbye and the other worthies of the Elizabethan age.'

5) *The Sleeper Wakened* is listed in White, *Register of First Performances*, as an opera; but *The Athenaeum* (20 October 1860 p.523) describes it as a 'Serenata' which might possibly be turned into an opera. Though the place of first performance was Her Majesty's Theatre, the occasion was a 'Grand National Concert', set up in rivalry to the monster concerts of Jullien.

6) *Morning Chronicle* 11 October 1860 p.3. Charles Pearce, p.226, explains that the 'Italian' part of Smith's scheme was made necessary by the refusal of Sims Reeves, who played Robin Hood, to sing more than three times a week. Reeves failed to fulfil his engagements as a matter of routine, and was absent from *Robin Hood* for a time owing to the death of his father.

7) The *Athenaeum* (29 September 1860 p.426) describes the extent of Smith's ambition: 'Mr Smith intends to have Italian operas at Liverpool and Manchester, moving about his company as suits him, and that there may be yet one more English operatic theatre in the building now called the Alhambra. All this, it will be at once perceived, savours of speculating monopoly more than Art. If Mr Smith, who is understood to have Drury Lane on his hands, cannot there establish English opera, or opera in English – neither at Her Majesty's Theatre more than three nights a week – how is an Alhambra opera to be manned and womanned, or fed with new English works, or old foreign works done into English? Another question: where are the orchestras to come from?'

8) Banister, *George Alexander Macfarren*, p.201.

9) Banister, *George Alexander Macfarren*, p.201.

10) *Robin Hood* was performed on Tuesday, Thursday and Saturday each week.

11) Santley, *Student and Singer*, p.172.

12) *Times* review 11 Nov 1861 p.4.

13) *The Era*, 27 April 1889. Performances took place on 29 April; 2 May; 4 May. *The Daily Telegraph* (6 May 1889 p.5) says the season lasted for three weeks, so more performances seem likely.

14) *The Times*: 6 and 10 August 1889.

15) *The Times* 15 October 1860, p.3.

16) *Morning Chronicle* 15 October 1860 p.3.

17) Oxenford, *Robin Hood*, p.31.

18) *Morning Chronicle* 15 October 1860 p.3.

19) *Athenaeum* 13 October 1860 p.488. The score was published virtually complete, but in separate numbers so that each could be purchased on an individual basis.

20) In addition to the score in separate numbers, a conventional vocal score, edited by Edward F. Rimbault, was also published. In reviewing this score the *Athenaeum* (20 October 1860 p.522/3) has a number of unkind things to say, including the following: 'Throughout this the folk's music has an uncouthness which, if it be the true old English tune, would make us wistfully long for new England.' The paper accuses Macfarren of deliberately going 'wrong' as a clumsy way of seeming unconventional.

21) *Robin Hood*, like *Lurline*, actually pre-dates the *Ring*, which first began to emerge in 1869.

BIBLIOGRAPHY

Banister, Henry Charles: *George Alexander Macfarren*; London, George Bell, 1891.

Oxenford, John: *Robin Hood, An Opera in Three Acts*; London, Brewer & Co. n.d. (1860).

Pearce, Charles E.: *Sims Reeves*; London, Stanley Paul, 1924.

Santley, Sir Charles: *Student and Singer*, London, Arnold, 1892.

Shaw, George Bernard: *Music in London* 1889-1889; London, Constable, 1937.

Shaw, George Bernard: *Shaw's Music*, Vol 2, 1890-1893; London, Bodley Head, 1981.

White, Eric Walter: *A Register of First Performances of English Operas*; London, Society for Theatre Research, 1983.

SCENE FROM *THE AMBER WITCH* – *Illustrated Times* 16 March 1866